To South Dakota and Back

The Story of the Great North American Harvest

By
Paul David Savage

Table of Contents

Whanganui, New Zealand
Houston, Texas, United States
April 2016. 1

Des Moines, Iowa
Litchfield, Minnesota
April 2016. 5

Litchfield, Minnesota
Superior, Nebraska
May 2016 21

Wichita Falls, Texas
May 2016 25

Kingman, Kansas
June 2016 48

Jewell, Kansas
June 2016 69

Eads, Colorado
June 2016 76

Onida, South Dakota
July 2016. 85

Regent, North Dakota
August 2016 95

Sturgis, South Dakota
August 2016 110

Regent, North Dakota
August 2016 115

Indian Head, Saskatchewan, Canada
September 2016 117

Onida, South Dakota, United States
September 2016 128

Minot, North Dakota
September 2016 131

Onida, South Dakota
September–October 2016 133

Annandale, Minnesota
October 2016 149

Des Moines, Iowa
October 2016 159

Epilogue 161

Thank You 163

About The Book 165

About the Author 166

Harvest Photo Album 167

Final Word 179

Whanganui, New Zealand
Houston, Texas, United States

"Uh ... Des Moines?" the travel agent asked. "Did you mean ... Detroit?" she queried.

"Um, no, I'd like to go to Des Moines, Iowa, please," I replied.

"Ok, Des Moines, sure," she confirmed. She looked as amused as she was curious. The giveaway was her Canadian accent. She knew where Des Moines was. She was probably wondering what on Earth a twenty-something in downtown Wellington, who had literally just walked in off the street, was doing asking to buy a plane ticket from Whanganui, New Zealand, to a city in the heart of the American Midwest. I didn't blame her.

In early 2016 I was working for the New Zealand Parliament in Wellington. I wrote speeches and gathered all sorts of information. I loved it. I had the best team out, I got on well with my bosses, and I got paid to write about interesting topics. It was a dream job and something I had wanted to do for a long time. The problem? I was losing my edge. I found myself drifting out of concentration

1

at times when I should not have. Silly errors crept into my work. I was regularly tiring out far quicker than a fit and healthy 27-year-old should. By that time I'd been part of the writing world for close to a decade. I knew I needed a bit of a breather so I could pick it up and run with it again in the future. A good month or few off in some far-away place drinking cocktails, riding motor scooters, and struggling to pronounce foreign words would probably have done the job. But I had other ideas.

A person wiser than me once said something along the lines of: 'the place your mind wanders to when it's idle is the place where you should be heading'. In my quieter moments, I would find myself thinking about driving tractors and combine harvesters. I asked around about it. I Googled it. It became very obvious very quickly. All roads with big farm machinery led to the United States and Canada. The home of John Deere, Case International Harvester (Case IH), Massey Ferguson, and all that good stuff that burns diesel. So what was it really like to live the harvesting life and experience it all for real? There was only one way to find out.

I got home from the gym one evening and tried my luck. I emailed a few harvest crews in the Midwestern United States. Within a day I had two job offers back. I accepted an offer to join a Minnesota-based custom harvesting crew set to travel all the way down to Texas, back up through the Midwest, over the border to Canada and back down to South Dakota. I gathered the necessary paperwork, got up to the United States Consulate in Auckland, and made it through what was a fairly painless visa process. Before I knew it, I was at home in the house I grew up in, packing my bags the morning after being the best man at the wedding of a very dear friend of mine, Waata. I placed on hold, indefinitely, a career I had spent a decade working to build up. I was about to fly around the world and do something completely different. What could possibly go wrong?

I said my goodbyes to Mum and Dad and flew the one-hour leg north from Whanganui to Auckland International Airport, New Zealand's gateway to the United States. After I'd checked in and passed security, I sat down and pulled out my recently-purchased iPad Mini. I knew within a month I'd be a harvest worker in northern Texas. And I knew I still didn't know how to play poker. I had confessed this to a work colleague about a week earlier. A seasoned poker weapon himself, the co-worker had kindly given me a crash-course on how not to get totally cleared out at the table. I figured with a fifteen-hour flight ahead of me, there was no time like the present to sharpen up and learn how to play the ever-famous poker variant, Texas hold 'em. What better time than on a direct flight to Houston, TX?

A few Four of a kinds, Full houses, and many folds later, my Air New Zealand flight touched down in Houston. Because I'd gone for a cheaper ticket on that long-haul flight I didn't get fed a lot. As soon as I cleared customs, I picked up my gear and dropped it on the carousel to be zipped off to the next plane, then I made a beeline for the food court. I annihilated a Whataburger combo and washed it down with a coffee from Starbucks. To me that seemed like an appropriate way to formally mark my first entry to the United States in almost eight years.

As I wandered around the airport, killing time, I noticed there weren't nearly as many Texan stereotypes as I had imagined. Apart from a woman who looked and sounded like Calleigh from *CSI: Miami*, most of the people walking around didn't sound distinctly Texan. I only saw one or two Stetson hats. There weren't many cowboy boots to go around, either. The Texan personalities I had pictured were burly, imposing figures who looked like Marcus Luttrell, Steve Austin, or Charles 'Charlie' Wilson. Airports can be transient sorts of places that don't always reflect the area in which they're located. At George Bush Intercontinental Airport that day, I wouldn't've known I was in Texas unless I looked at the location on my phone. It wasn't a let-down. It just wasn't quite what I had imagined.

Three hours later it was time to board the plane to Des Moines, Iowa. The aircraft was a small propeller plane, which meant that we had to walk out onto the tarmac instead of filing down the usual jet bridge. It was hot outside. I guessed it was about 100. That suited me just fine. As much as I missed the winter rugby season at home in New Zealand, with it came a bitter cold that dragged on for several unrelenting months. The sweltering Texan heat was a welcome change for me. Besides, I'd never functioned well in the cold—I much prefer the heat. What to expect at our destination? I didn't really know. Des Moines was a blank canvas to me. I knew Stone Sour and Bill Bryson came from Des Moines. I knew there was corn, lots of it, growing on the limitless farmland that surrounded it. That didn't sound so bad to me at all. Bring on the Hawkeyes!

Des Moines, Iowa
Litchfield, Minnesota

April 2016

It was time to get to work. My bus up-state from Des Moines to St. Cloud, Minnesota, wasn't due to leave for a couple of hours. I'd ordered a wake-up call from the hotel reception, just in case I slept through my alarm. The cab driver who took me to the Greyhound bus terminal was a Vietnam War veteran. When he heard my accent, he recounted his trips to Kings Cross and the Sydney city surrounds back in his day. It was the second time in as many days I'd been mistaken for an Australian.

The 'Aussie' Australian accent is not a world away from the 'Kiwi' New Zealand accent. That's why the mistake made abroad confusing the two has never wound me up. That said, I don't have a particularly strong Kiwi accent. Distinguishing an Aussie from a Kiwi is not easy for the untrained ear, especially not in a corner of the world that seldom hears what a New Zealander sounds like. I view this commonly-made mistake as a great conversation-starter—not something to get all upset and dramatic about, as a determined handful of Kiwis make a habit of doing.

As daylight broke on the trip north, I spent the whole time staring out the window at every passing farm. The place was flat. So flat. I couldn't get over it. I'd heard stories and I'd read all about it. Seeing it in real life was an entirely different matter. My home region in New Zealand, Manawatu-Wanganui, has some flatter sections. None of it was as ironing-table-like as what I saw out the window. About an hour into the bus trip we pulled in to a blink-and-you'll-miss-it town for a comfort stop at a Burger King and gas station complex. I contemplated making a run for it to grab a hash brown and a coffee. The problem was, the bus driver didn't say how long we were going to sit around for, and he left the engine running. Also, I didn't like the idea of my first phone call to my new boss being one to inform him that I'd missed the bus and gotten left behind because I wanted a feed.

Following a bus transfer at Saint Paul, MN, and after another hour on the road, I made it to St. Cloud, MN. It struck me as a fairly pleasant city—except, it was cold! Far too cold for a person who's made for warm weather, and who was only wearing a work shirt and a Caterpillar-branded hoodie that did nothing to stop the breeze coming through. Fortunately, a man in a John Deere hoodie walked over to me and asked if I was Paul. He said he had the car waiting. I'd have told him my name was Alice if it meant getting out of that bitter cold for a few moments.

After only a minute or so of chat, it was clear I was in good company. Devin, the man who'd come to collect me, was another one of the Holland Harvesting crew members who'd journeyed to the United States from overseas. A strongly built individual with an equally broad accent to boot, he'd traveled from an area just inland from Durban, South Africa. Devin gave me a quick run-down of the operation so far and what to expect back at the farm.

I recognized the place from photos I'd seen on Google satellite view as Devin pulled the Lincoln Town Car into the driveway. I'd finally made it to Holland Harvesting headquarters. Located on a 250-acre farm property about fifteen minutes from Litchfield, MN, it was flat, surrounded by trees, and very green. The scene perfectly resembled the image of Minnesota I had imagined. But this was no time to stand by and take in the sights. I threw down my gear on an unattended bunk bed in the crew quarters, chucked my work gear on, and headed over to the workshop to get amongst it.

The Holland Harvesting setup was impressive. The main shed and workshop area had the tools, devices, and implements for all kinds of jobs. It even had heated floors. The only farm machinery visible was a bunch of brand spanking new Case IH combine harvesters and tractors. They looked great. But there was a problem. The machines were not green and yellow. In that workshop, there was a distinct lack of John Deere, my much-loved manufacturer of farm machinery, and Case IH's biggest rival. That was no great surprise. Going to a Case IH-equipped outfit and expecting to find a John Deere machine is like going to a Burger King restaurant and hoping to get yourself a Big Mac. It isn't going to happen. And you might be asked to leave.

The guys were busy going about a bunch of tasks. I joined in, helped where I could, and introduced myself along the way. The crew that had already gathered at HQ was a mix of Americans and overseas imports. I met Clint, a metal worker and generally handy individual from across in Covington, Indiana. Clint was knowledgeable on all things military, firearms, knives, metal, and anything with a combustion engine. There was John, a diesel mechanic from the Fargo-Moorhead area, Minnesota. A keen Snap-On tool enthusiast and hydraulics whizz, John offered intricately detailed descriptions of engine and gearbox components, how things worked, and consistent, well-timed references to the TV show *South Park*.

I met Cory, a truck driver and keen sports pundit from Aurora, Colorado. Cory shared much of my taste in music. He was always up for a chat about anything from working in the oilfields, our shared Christian faith, and more. A former United States Marine, Cory was always interesting to listen to and learn from. Then there was George, a truck driver and former custom harvest crew owner-operator himself from McDonald, Kansas. A long-time contemporary of Rob Holland, our boss, George was a relaxed and gently-spoken individual. But, with several decades of harvest and farm work under his belt, and despite the years of age he had on us twenty-somethings, George still had the build and strength to throw a much younger man out the window just as easily as he might ask them if they could pass him a ¾ drive wrench. Cory and George would serve as the crew foremen for Harvest 2016.

Then there was Cassie, a truck driver, and farmhand from the Eastern Cape of South Africa. Cassie had a wild, sarcastic sense of humor and delivered jokes only he could make funny. He was a scream. I also met Tony, a farm manager and machinery operator from England's East Midlands region. Tony would help me out and offer helpful guidance all throughout the season with a generous dollop of his English-style humor. There was also Tommy, the resident mechanic, from Centerville, Tennessee. Tommy liked John Deere, diesel engines, and sweet tea. Tommy's choice of movies and books pretty much aligned with mine. Lastly, there was Kelvin, an Australian, from Oakey, Queensland. His parents ran a custom harvesting outfit. I bet all the crew wondered where on Earth the speechwriter from New Zealand was supposed to fit in. I can tell you, I sure did!

Our mission for the season was to harvest a whole lot of grain, seeds, beans, and kernels. The arrangement was straightforward. Farmers would hire our bosses, the business founders and co-owners Rob and Sue Holland, to take care of harvesting and hauling their crop. The farmer supplied the land and the plants. Rob, and his wife, Sue, supplied the machinery and the crew to operate it. As a crew, we'd move the haul trucks, combine harvesters, grain carts, service trucks, and anything else we might need. We'd head to a farm, harvest and haul the crop, then up sticks and move on to the next place. We would be hired guns on the run. We were to travel to Texas, up through the Midwest, back up to the Canada–United States border, cross over it, and come back again to the United States for the fall harvest. I'd seen clips on YouTube, read accounts of it all on online forums, and chatted to a couple of guys who'd done it. The common theme was that to really understand it, you had to do it.

Come supper time, I was starving. There was fried chicken on the menu and plenty of it. I did a lot more listening and eating than I did talking during that supper. When we were done, I heard there was a trip to the local Walmart happening that evening. I'd also heard earlier in the day that every person on the crew should carry his or her own knife on their person. When I asked whether it was for practical use—cutting twine, plastic, and so forth—or for personal protection, I was told, with a mischievous grin, "both". Whatever the real reason was, I didn't care. I wanted in on it. I asked Clint if I'd be able to get this much-needed knife at Walmart. Clint just looked over at me and said: "If Walmart doesn't have it, you don't need it!" Clint had a deadpan style of delivering what he had to say. He also resembled a younger David Morse. For that reason, and as we were about to go out looking for a bunch of sharp knives, I tried to think of anything other than the film *Disturbia*.

9

The nearby town, Litchfield, fit many of the small-town Midwest stereotypes that popular culture had fed me. It had a big highway section going through the middle. Lots of semi-trucks rolled past. There were the usual fast food outlets. There were green parks, trees, and farm machinery dealerships. We saw a National Guard Armory (complete with a sign pointing to it), and billboards with local high school and community information on them. And, of course, there was a Walmart. All I knew of Walmart was the peculiar Facebook page 'Humans of Walmart' that featured all kinds of strange. The reality was, Walmart certainly did have a lot of stuff. It didn't take me long to find a camouflage-patterned folding knife.

When we got back to HQ, I found I was a bit late to the party on getting a good pillow. I rigged a makeshift one with some of my clean gear. Our crew quarters consisted of a 'trailer', the American term for a rectangular-shaped house that was probably towed to its final location. A bit dated inside and out, and nestled behind the workshop amongst a bunch of trees and some seriously green grass, the trailer was our home for the time we were at HQ. Our trailer was comfortable, and it certainly had character. But, most importantly, it was warm. That was what really mattered in the cool, late-April Minnesota air. After I sorted out my sleep and storage spaces, I ventured out into the lounge. All the guys had claimed their nightly spots on the numerous couches, chairs, and objects scattered throughout the room.

I got chatting away with John about cars, farm machines, and our shared enthusiasm for *South Park*. John asked me, "Why are John Deere's colors green and yellow?"

I replied, genuinely not knowing the answer to his question, "Uh I don't know man, why?"

John advised me, "It's so they can hide in the daisies when the Case IH comes into the field."

I didn't really know what to make of it. My laughter was authentic. I had taken part in my fair share of farm machinery banter over time. I'd said some fairly colorful things about rival brands to my friends to get under their skin. But John's quip? Well, I'd never heard that one! I was only a day into our great journey. I knew already: it was going to be a wild ride with a great bunch of guys.

The next morning, I made an important discovery. Each day would begin with a fresh pot of 'filter' coffee on the drip. Filter coffee is a yesteryear relic in New Zealand. The last time it was popular there would have been about the time when Ronald Reagan was the President of the United States. In the trailer, it was a pleasant sight to witness the drip going early in the morning so we could be readily caffeinated for a day's work.

That morning we got busy working on the grain cart, a large trailer that's towed behind the tractor. The grain cart operator's job is to run around the field and collect the harvested product from the combine harvesters and take it to the semi-trucks. More about that later. I undid the grain cart's firehose and proceeded to wreck it in the process. Kelvin and Cory reassured a somewhat stunned and sheepish me that it could be easily fixed. That hose looked like it hadn't been unwound for a long time. We hit the tools and went about mending it.

Following another day of spinning spanners, we made a repeat run to Litchfield. I tried my luck with a *Family-Guy*-themed state lottery ticket and netted myself a cool ten-dollar prize. Immediately after this successful gambling trip to Econofoods, John introduced me to the Midwest wonder that is Dairy Queen. I spent far too long going over every option on the menu board before settling on the infamous Blizzard. It was a real treat. I was hooked.

Early the next morning, Sue sent me and Kelvin down the road to St. Cloud with Clint so we could get our Social Security numbers. Sue Holland is the archetypal 'camp mom' figure. She'd employed and been in charge of ambitious, over-confident young men for decades. As a real mother, too, she really had seen and heard it all. Sue's demeanor always made it clear she wouldn't take crap from anyone. Her straightforward, business-like approach to things aside, she was always there in the operation as someone to look out for you when you needed it most. Sue hired, fired, cooked, shot, drove trucks, combined, and pulled many a young buck into line with her dour version of humor when required. Sue is a treasure.

It was in the St. Cloud Social Security office where I saw my first pistol in the United States, holstered on the waist of a security guard. I also saw a sign on the wall reminding Social Security Number applicants that, as they were in a federal building, they were not allowed to carry a weapon of any sort. I did my best to block out any questions as to whether or not I still had my knife in my pocket. After we got our numbers done up, we ventured over the road and hit Arby's with Clint. A local kid heard us talking, came over, and said he really wanted to visit Australia. He told us he knew of the late Steve Irwin. Kelvin and I smiled. Then we both told him, "Good on ya, mate." The fact that kid thought we were both Australian was not lost on Kelvin. I'm sure he enjoyed that.

Following another day of hitting the tools in the workshop, I decided to strike out for a walk in the evening. I have led an active lifestyle since the word go. Strolling around to get the feel of a new place, if it isn't too dodgy, is a favored pastime of mine. Out in rural Litchfield there weren't a lot of footpaths. But the roads were nice and wide, and because most vehicles out there were pickup trucks and SUVs, you could spot them a mile away. Because of those big wide roads, I never felt unsafe walking on an unsealed road where vehicles regularly hit at least forty miles per hour.

On the first Saturday that rolled around, a few of us were tasked with a mission to head up to an RV (recreational vehicle) store to collect a few provisions for the upcoming harvest. I paused to think for a moment. One of the guys said we were headed somewhere called 'Pleasureland'. I figured that in a cut-and-dried area of the Midwest there was probably some sort of explanation for a place that sounded like it might have been in the business of selling things other than RV parts. As it turned out, Pleasureland was in fact the name of the RV shop. Once we found the required parts, we had a good look around at the outstanding model selection in the yard.

The place had all kinds of fifth-wheel, tow-behind and self-propelled RVs. Acres of them. It also had a selection of Ford F-series pickups and a handful of Chevrolet Corvettes for sale, which I spent a while checking out. Alongside Pleasureland ran the Interstate 94 (I-94) Highway. I walked over to the fence and spent a few minutes watching the Interstate commuters. It was novel. I've liked cars since I could crawl. I enjoyed standing there, watching those great big American Camaros, Tahoes and Raptors fly on by. They're fine automobiles that are seldom found in New Zealand.

Supper that night was a bunch of American stereotypes jam-packed into one. After we'd been to Walmart so I could grab a pillow, the Americans—John, Tommy, and Clint—suggested we hit Texas Roadhouse to eat. That sounded like a brilliant idea if ever I'd heard one. There was no argument from Kelvin, either. I will never forget walking into Texas Roadhouse in St. Cloud, MN, that night. There were old-school neon beer sign lights. There were cowboy hats and boots. There were fresh cuts of meat ready to be served. Country music was playing. It was a Saturday night, and boy, that place was *hopping*. Looking back, that was really was my 'Welcome to America, this is what it's all about' moment. I glanced at Kelvin. I didn't say a word. I smiled and nodded twice. He did the same. We both knew there was no doubt we'd hit the epicenter of Uncle Sam's country.

After we took our seats, we were given a basket of unshelled peanuts. I stared at them for a moment. Not John. He dove straight in, shelled a peanut like a seasoned pro and tossed the remains over his shoulder onto the floor. He must've seen the shock on my face. John promptly grabbed me a few peanuts, banged me on the shoulder and reassured me, "It's what you're meant to do here!" I followed suit before ordering an 8oz steak with chips, some corn, and a Bud Light on tap—the beer that would remain my go-to choice of on-tap beverage throughout our travels.

One of the many things I noticed that night was how many men wore caps and headwear at the dinner table. They were labeled with everything from Cummins Diesel to Caterpillar, Farmall, Case IH, Under Armour and John Deere. In the Midwest, the women wore caps a lot, too, except I didn't see them bring them to supper very often. The girls tended to stick with them for outdoors work, but not for meal times. Machinery operators and grain farmers often wear baseball caps and trucker hats. In New Zealand, even at a restaurant in the provinces, most guys will remove their caps or hats at dinner time. But, over there in the Midwest, a cap was pretty much standard issue. It worked for me!

When we arrived back at the trailer that night we met Jake, the newest addition to the crew. A genial, machinery-loving country boy and recently-licensed truck driver from fifty minutes out of Memphis, Tennessee, Jake had an accent straight out of a film. Minutes later, when we got talking machinery, I asked him about the CVT transmission setup on the tractors we would be running. His reply? "Just put her in gear, bad bitch pretty much drive herself!" Laugh as I did, I later found out Jake's description was in fact very accurate, although I'm sure the Case IH brochures and sales representatives word the description a little differently.

As the days passed in the workshop, I began to settle a little more. I tried my hand at as many tasks as I could. I dug rows for potatoes, carved out pipe trenches with Rob in the alfalfa field, moved around trucks for servicing, and I had a blast on the Holland's ride-on lawnmower. To my delight, it was a John Deere. I should note that in many southern and Midwestern states, John Deere has a strong hold on the lawn tractor (ride-on lawnmower) market. Those little green machines were *everywhere.*

While I was cutting the grass I saw a dead snake. It alarmed me for a moment, even though I was piloting the trusty John Deere and was therefore safely out of the serpent's attacking range. Until then, I had never seen a snake outside the confines of a reptile enclosure at a zoo. I mentioned it to the guys after supper, only to be reminded: "Remember—the more southern it gets, the nastier the snakes become!" I didn't diary it, but I'm sure it was Tommy who said that. I knew full well there were snakes in the United States. Seeing one up close in the wild was a timely reminder—the threat was real!

Our day-to-day work setting was pleasant. Minnesota was pretty at that time of year. The weather and temperature were relatively mild. The Holland Harvesting HQ featured lots of trees, big and small. They surrounded the workshop building, trailer, and other sheds, and they backed on to the fields of alfalfa crop and sections of extraordinarily green grass. We barely saw a car or truck pass by on the adjacent rural road. As far as work locations went, you could do a lot worse that what we had.

At night after work we would typically sit around and drink beer and 'pop'. Pop is Midwestern for what a New Zealander would call a soft drink, like Coca-Cola or Sprite. We'd watch whatever was on TV and just chat. As the nights got warmer, we migrated to the porch out back. Out there one night I sat with Jake and had a good yarn. Jake reclined, pulled out a tin of tobacco and started to go to work on it. I caught his eye, held the glance, looked at the tin, and looked up at Jake. I said, "Sir, d'ya mind if I give that a whirl? I've never had it before." The variety of tobacco prepared and sold for chewing is not readily available in New Zealand. You're allowed to bring some back from abroad, but you certainly can't go down to the corner store and buy yourself a tin of it.

Jake, without hesitation, said, "Sure, go right ahead." I fished out a wad and got ready to lodge it in between my jaw and lip. Before I did, I hesitated.

I looked at Jake and asked, "So how much are you meant to put there?"

He smiled, threw his head back and responded, "As much as y'all want, big guy."

I threw in the moderate amount I'd grabbed and waited to see what would happen. The stuff got to me pretty quick. My head felt a little light, and I'm pretty sure my blood ran through my upper body a little faster than usual.

Jake laughed and said, "You enjoying yourself over there?"

I lay back a bit further, nodded, and confirmed, "Yep. Sure am!"

With the departure for Texas imminent, our daily tasks moved from machinery maintenance to readying and detailing (polishing and cleaning) vehicles for the road. I spent a good chunk of one morning refueling with Cory. As we chatted away, I mentioned my admiration for the center consoles found in American vehicles.

Those things were seriously impressive. Even in a smaller car, you'd have room for your wallet, phone, drink, and whatever other small articles you would carry with you in the car, such as a bag of sunflower seeds. In the pickup trucks, the center consoles were even bigger. I would later have this same conversation with Kelvin, who agreed the North American console examples were something to write home about.

A couple of days later, Rob needed eager and willing volunteers to get on his workshop roof and see to a bit of guttering that needed a touch-up. I pretended I was both those things and volunteered. About half-way up the machine lift to the top, I knew it was a bad decision. I hate heights. I instantly regretted it. I could've stuck with washing trucks or detailing the pickups back on solid ground, but instead, I'd ended up at roof level with Cassie, the devilish practical joker. As I leaned out to apply the sealant to the leaky spots, Cassie managed to shake the back of my platform. It wasn't enough to endanger me, but it was certainly enough to know he'd frightened the hell out of me. I threatened him with grievous bodily harm if he didn't stop his tomfoolery immediately. Of course, he stopped. Then he shook the platform again when I turned the other way only minutes later. Cassie's contagious laughter just made it too hard to get annoyed with him.

Shortly before we rolled out to Texas, I went for another countryside walk. It turned out to be a walk I will never forget. It was a sunny, warm Sunday afternoon. We had an hour or two to kill before supper. In the United States I'd always walk on the left-hand side of the road because in America, you drive on the right-hand side of the road. That way, if a car was coming towards me I'd see it and move. Likewise, if a car was approaching from behind, it would miss me by several feet. As I wandered along that dusty Minnesota road, I saw a woman cutting the grass on a John Deere lawn tractor. She was wearing an outdoors work shirt and a pair of shorts that were not very long. She wore no shoes or sunglasses. She was strikingly attractive. And she was operating a John Deere. I knew it was an image I would struggle to get rid of.

I continued my stroll and got closer. The woman pulled the John Deere up within a few feet of me and said, with a smile that was a mile wide, "Hi, how are ya?" I swear that 'Hi' was dragged out that little bit longer.

"Never better! How about you, ma'am?" I replied.

"I'm good," she said, nodded, and smiled, "you take care now."

As I walked back to Holland Harvesting HQ, I concluded the breathtaking John Deere operator was a daughter back home from college or some other place. I ran some opening lines through my head. The sort of 'Hi, I'm new to the Midwest, and I'm from New Zealand, so how are ya?' types, and how to not make it obvious to the rest of the crew that I would probably go for another walk that way. When I got back to the trailer I did a quick round of Facebook investigating. I discovered it wasn't the daughter I'd run into. It was the mom. I decided any future plans I had should probably stop right there and then.

It was also then, all of a sudden, that a conversation I'd had with Rob earlier in the day made sense. Rob generally gave instructions and asked questions in two ways. His first and most common method was straightforward and brief. He'd tell you what he wanted, where he wanted it, and how he wanted it done. Rob seldom wasted words. You generally weren't left wondering what he was after. His second, less common method involved a deadpan expression, unseen or unexplained references, and his heavy Minnesotan accent.

That Sunday afternoon when I was headed out of the yard on my walk, Rob asked if I was planning on moving in a particular direction toward a certain location. I told Rob yes, I was planning on heading that way. He said, "Well don't you go too far in at that place there, they might get the shotgun out." I'd owned shotguns for years. I'd blasted plenty of clay pigeons in my time. I didn't fancy taking a round of steel-shot to the chest. I told Rob I wouldn't. There was a hint of a smile on Rob's face when he said "Ok". At the time I didn't get the full picture. I thought, maybe, he meant a general word of caution about not trespassing, given a lot of rural Midwesterners owned guns. I didn't know. About half an hour later, after that lawn tractor encounter, I was pretty sure I knew exactly what Rob was getting at.

Only days out from our trip south, we claimed spots in our home for the next six months: the crew trailer. The crew trailer was a semi-trailer which would be hauled by a Kenworth T800 truck unit wherever we went. It slept eight guys in two four-bunk rooms and came complete with a small kitchen and combined lounge area, including a TV. With the seven occupants it ended up with, the crew trailer was always going to be somewhat cramped. But I had to say, I thought it was all good. I grabbed some of my gear and claimed a top bunk that had a slightly enclosed headspace. It appealed to me because it had more storage room for books and my iPad. If anyone wasn't sure which space was mine, they would be soon enough. I marked it with my Tom Clancy novel—*Clear and Present Danger*— my desert camouflaged hat, my Hurricanes rugby shirt, and my bag of sunflower seeds.

The night before we rolled out, Cory pulled us aside and gave us all a briefing of what to expect on the road down. An ex-Marine, Cory had a clear-cut, to-the-point way of giving out directions to the group as if we were his fire team. I wasn't concerned about the length of the drive. But I was a little edgy about what might happen if a county sheriff or state trooper got any ideas and decided to pull me over for a little one-on-one. I was assured I'd likely be fine, and my New Zealand license should keep me from any real trouble. I had actually passed my Minnesota driver's license exam a few days earlier, but the proof hadn't arrived in the mail yet. I'll admit, I was a little nervous, but I was pretty excited at the same time. I had stocked up with some snacks for the road and, of course, a fresh bag of sunflower seeds.

Six combine harvesters, two grain carts, and several trucks are quite a bit of iron and steel to move around. To move all our machinery took at least two trips. Rob, Cory, and George had already made a trip to the Lone Star State with several machines by the time the rest of the crew was ready to move out from Minnesota. This pattern would continue throughout the season. When we were headed to a new farm, or state, a smaller group of trucks and trailers would move out with the first load of gear. When the drivers returned, we'd all move as a grand, almighty convoy. That time had come. In the morning, it was off to the races.

Litchfield, Minnesota
Superior, Nebraska

May 2016

"This is it. This is what you all came here for," Rob said. It was moving day. We were off. The mood that morning was buzzing. We'd loaded our machinery in the days before. We all knew who would be driving what, with whom, and to where. We were well prepared. Except for Rob, Sue, and George, no-one on the crew had lived the full Harvest America experience front to back. We were itching to go at it. My mission was simple: I would be co-driving with Clint in the Lincoln Town Car. One of us would take the wheel and the other would operate the two-way radio. We fired up our engines, checked our radios and rolled out of town. Destination: Wichita Falls, TX. Nearly a thousand miles away.

About half an hour into the journey, we pulled into a gas station so the truck drivers could check their vehicles. A lot of Midwest gas stations have a large gravel area out the back for that very purpose. I helped Kelvin look over his truck, which seemed to be behaving itself, before we headed inside. In the harvesting world, you quickly learned to make the most of any opportunity to sleep, use the bathroom, or grab food and drink. You didn't always know when your next stop was going to be. It might not be for another 15 hours or more. When I'd grabbed a can of my trusty Monster Energy Coffee, a favorite of mine back home before it was discontinued, I looked over some of the bumper stickers on sale. Political correctness was not really an in-thing in that end of town. Some of the stickers were absolute pearlers. 'Put on yo' big girl pants and DEAL WITH IT' and 'Diesel fumes make me horny, baby' were a couple of the more memorable examples. A couple of us agreed the latter sticker's text sounded better read aloud with Tommy and Jake's Tennessee accents.

Not long after our gas station pit-stop, we crossed the western Minnesota state line into South Dakota. I recognized the Mount Rushmore design on the license plates I'd seen earlier on, complete with the *Great Faces. Great Places.* slogan. I'd talked to a couple of South Dakota residents who were in Minnesota the week beforehand. They'd told me that South Dakota was an attractive place, financially speaking, to reside. I heard taxation was not something the state was big on, and, if I was looking for a Midwest state to call home, South Dakota was a good start. While the idea of lower taxes was enticing, South Dakota looked to me, on my first impression, like a heck of a nice place to be. And, there were churches. Churches everywhere. You name the denomination, we would've driven past half a dozen of its places of worship. Except Anglican, my denomination. No surprises there!

Steeples aside, I saw more farm machinery and implements than I had in my life. Every small town in South Dakota seemed to come with its own dealership and selection of big iron. It's common knowledge that agriculture keeps the lights on in South Dakota, but to appreciate the scale of the machinery needed to get the job done, it's a real 'see it is to believe it' kind of deal. In New Zealand, a lot of farming doesn't need tractors with more than 200 or so horsepower. In South Dakota—well, there weren't many farms we passed that didn't have a 400+ horsepower machine working the ground or standing by ready to go. An hour or so later we crossed a long causeway section over the Missouri River. It didn't look unlike bits of the Rangitikei River crossing near Bulls, back in New Zealand, except it was all on a big slope. The far end of the crossing marked my first entry to the state of Nebraska.

I'd always heard Nebraska was flat. The part of it we went through had a fair bit of country that wasn't flat at all. It was green and rugged. I voiced this to Clint, who correctly pointed out that we'd caught some of the rougher parts of the state, and that there was still plenty of flat areas to go around. I don't think we drove through the part of Nebraska that was the basis for the film *Children of the Corn*. Although it was set in Nebraska, I would later find out that much of it was filmed over in Iowa. The word going around on our two-way radio was that storms were forecast. I looked around for a tornado lifting up a house, only to see a few dark clouds on the horizon. We'd recently swapped drivers, so with Clint at the wheel, I got busy ripping into the sunflower seeds and taking in the countryside views.

I had a good yarn with Clint in the car that day. Clint fielded all my questions, of which there were many, and gave candid answers. He discussed life in the Midwest, the state of Indiana, and the obvious and unseen differences between the north-lying and southern states. He told me about what many consider to be 'southern' in terms of culture, dress, cuisine, music, and more. He discussed recent and distant historical events from an American perspective. It was refreshing to hear a local, unfiltered take on things from a born-and-bred citizen. It was a far cry from the sanitized, opinion-soaked version that often makes its way to the far end of the world via edited news stories and conveniently-cut social media clips. During those few hours with Clint, I learned more about the inner workings of the United States of America than I had in my entire life.

We ended a good day behind the wheel at Superior, NE, a town that lies about a mile north of the Nebraska-Kansas state line. Superior was not an unpleasant place, but I suspect its name might have created a few unrealistic expectations. After finding a spot to park up the trailers, trucks, and a dash to the gas station to get some fuel, we made ourselves at home in a Pizza Hut. Rob wasted no time in ordering supper. When Kelvin, our resident Australian, asked for a pizza with chicken on it, Rob looked at Kelvin as if he'd asked for an overnight repeal of the Second Amendment. I quietly shared Kelvin's enthusiasm for an avian-featured pizza suggestion. An assortment of pizzas promptly arrived. There wasn't a hungry belly left in the house.

Although we didn't have power and water going in our trailer, I think the general feeling was we were all relieved to get some shut-eye. There was a big day ahead and everybody knew it. I played a few revision hands of Texas hold 'em on the iPad and fell asleep in minutes.

Wichita Falls, Texas

May 2016

In the morning we woke up and got a move on. We had places to be and people to see. By 6:30 am we were on the road and headed south. I was new to Nebraskan geography, but Clint, a good judge of his home Midwest region, estimated we weren't far off the Nebraska–Kansas state line. We didn't have good reception the night before, so that was an educated guess, as we didn't know exactly where we were at that time. Clint was right. We'd barely come out of our sleep by the time we made it to Kansas. First stop: Jewell.

Jewell is a sleepy little town right up in the central northern area of Kansas. I don't recall if I knew at the time, but later on we would return to Jewell to harvest up a storm. In central Jewell, there were old Dodge pickup trucks rolling around, kids being dropped off for the school bus, and lots of people waving to each other. No-one was in a hurry. No-one looked too wound up, and no-one seemed to go about their business without saying 'hi' and acknowledging their neighbors and passers-by. Jewell is a salt-of-the-Earth, small American town.

Kansas is *flat*. As we headed along the highway south, I peered out the window at what looked like seemingly endless wheat. The sky looked bigger than ever before. There was more wheat out there than you could even Photoshop. Apart from the sky and the crops, the only other thing visible was one of the handful of lone oil pumpjacks scattered throughout the landscape. I knew there was oil further south; I had no idea that Kansas was in on it too. On the road through the Sunflower State, Clint told me about the now-famous study that found Kansas really was flatter than a pancake. It would've taken a brave person to step outside and try to convince those around them that the study got it wrong.

We pushed south. The next state down was Oklahoma, the Sooner State. It was America on meth. Everywhere I turned I saw Jeep Wranglers, Ram pickup trucks, fast food joints, and signs with the names of past Presidents. We'd barely broken out of Kansas and already the scene was changing faster than a Chevrolet Corvette at full noise. Everything, and I mean *everything*, in the place seemed to have this film of ochre dust covering it. As far as I knew we weren't going to be doing any harvesting in Oklahoma, so I seized the opportunity to take in as much of it as I could from the road south. To add to the Murica vibe of Oklahoma, I received a long, loud blast of the horn from a Halliburton-marked oil truck. I believe I was well into that driver's lane, so I therefore deserved the earful I copped from that giant, red-colored beast.

A little while later, we pulled up next to a big, bullish-looking, long-nosed truck tractor unit towing a semi-trailer. It was a stunning bit of gear. I thought it looked like a custom-built truck for a film. I gestured toward it and asked Clint about it. He told me it was a Peterbilt 379, "A very Midwestern truck," as he described it. On our drive south I noticed more and more of these models, as well as the similar-looking Kenworth W900 model.

Many of these trucks had loud engine brakes. These 'Jake brakes', or simply 'Jakes', got their name from the company called Jacobs

Vehicle Systems. The Jake brake setup works by retarding the truck's engine to slow the vehicle so the driver can control and maintain its speed, as opposed to using brake pads (service brakes). The Jakes work by popping open the engine's exhaust valves right after its compression stroke. The release of the compressed air from within the cylinders produces a sound for the ages. Depending on the engine and exhaust setup, it sounds something like clattering metal or a large-caliber machine gun firing. That sound would become par for the course in rural United States on Harvest 2016. Better still, some of these trucks were fitted with 'straight pipe' exhaust systems. The straight pipe setup has no catalytic converter, muffler, or restriction on air flow between the motor and the exhaust tip. The result was a thunderously loud chorus that could be heard from miles away. It was a thing of beauty. It was the song of our people!

We crossed the state line into Texas near a place called Burkburnett. To me, that just *sounded* like a place from Texas. It looked like it, too. The roads were big and wide—namely the adjacent Interstate 44 Highway—and there were livestock trailers everywhere. Many of them were hauled by Peterbilts and hulking, long-nosed Kenworth models. They were fitted with leering, bullhorn-style or sky-scraping straight pipe exhaust stacks. Patriotic stickers and flags adorned the GMC, Dodge, and Chevrolet pickups and SUVs that owned the roads. I already knew it was my kind of place.

The first port of call was a yard we called Helena. It's a chemical storage depot where custom cutters (a colloquial industry term for custom harvesters) could park up their machines. It took its name from the Helena agricultural chemical firm. Helena is a large, dirt lot right by Interstate 44 with a bunch of mobile anhydrous ammonia tanks sitting around, right behind a John Deere dealership, Quality Implement Co. When you're party to a crew moving several trucks

27

at a time, 'parking up' is a lot easier said than done. In previous days, there had clearly been rain. My mission was to make sure I didn't put the Lincoln in a mud patch, which, within seconds, I almost managed to do. I was just waiting for someone to turn around and yell out: "Paul, dammit, Kiwi—you had *ONE JOB!*"

Once we'd unloaded the lion's share of our machinery, we headed a few miles down the road to camp. Our site was right in the middle of a local wheat farm near Iowa Park, not far from a drag racing strip and, as I later found out, a maximum security prison. We got busy setting up. This involved reversing in the crew trailer, leveling it, hooking up the power and water supplies and, at Rob's request, placing pool noodle foam on the edges of the trailer's protruding slider, a section that extends out to broaden the floor area.

Rob said that, in the dark, it was all too easy to run straight into one of those unforgiving bits of metal on the edge of the slide-out section. With some height on me and a newly found overenthusiasm for Texas, I couldn't help think Rob was suggesting I would be a prime suspect for head-butting one of the edges myself. I took the hint and applied the foam guards. Like the Helena lot, our campsite had some water on the ground. The warning was spread: watch out for snakes. We were definitely in 'rattler' country.

By the time we'd set up camp, we were all pretty hungry. It was the sort of hunger that crept up on you, because in the hours beforehand you were too busy driving and working to think about nutrition. George called out and rounded us up for supper. We climbed into the two bright red, Holland Harvesting-marked Dodge Ram 2500 Laramie pickups and headed for Braum's, an ice cream shop and burger joint found in the southern United States. The staff were polite and welcoming, and the food was excellent. It was a nice welcome to Texas. To top it off, Rob said we could sleep until he woke us the next morning.

It rained hard overnight. In the crew trailer, I was in the top bunk, where I remained throughout the season. My head would rest about a foot below the roof of the trailer. If it rained, boy did I know all about it up there. We were allowed to sleep until just after 8 am. In the harvest world, that's a mighty fine sleep-in. Small lakes had formed outside our trailer and all around the campsite. As you stepped out the door you had to be careful you didn't go for a swim before breakfast.

We'd made it to Texas. The real work was set to kick off soon. But, the crew needed lunch provisions. We headed out. Where else but Walmart! That Walmart Supercenter north of Wichita Falls, just south of Sheppard Air Force Base, perfectly illustrated the stark contrast between a southern state and an upper Midwestern state. Back at the Minnesota Walmart in Litchfield, MN, there was a more than adequate delicatessen and hot-food section. In the Texas Walmart, there were *whole sections* dedicated to pizza, Mexican food, and fried chicken. In Minnesota, the snack aisle was well-stocked. In Texas, it was a matter of choosing *which* snack aisle you to walk down. And, in Minnesota, you could get yourself a gas-powered BB pistol. In Texas, you could buy a shotgun. The saying doesn't lie. Everything is bigger in Texas.

Even though the rain had bucketed down overnight and we weren't quite ready to mount the machinery and get cutting, there were still fields that needed to be checked. Rob was going to take one of the pickups out to have a look. I tagged along with him and Tony. I was eager to build on my bank of grain harvesting knowledge which, then, amounted to about nothing. We ventured out into a field just behind Interstate 44 that extended close to the edge of Sheppard Air Force Base, an installation that hosted a training programme for NATO-nation pilots.

The spot where we checked out the wheat was comfortably clear of the base fence. Still, we were probably closer to the edge of it than most people were allowed. I'm sure we didn't bother the airfield guards, but I wasn't keen to find out what happened if I went any closer. I did pay close attention to the condition of the wheat—it was good, but wasn't quite ready—but I couldn't help but gawk at the angular, nimble aircraft jetting around the Texan sky. New Zealand canned its air fighter wing in 2001, so seeing a small trainer jet that looked like a fighter plane zooming around was a real treat for an expatriate Kiwi enthusiastic about aircraft.

That night I got myself acquainted with another southern treat: iced tea. I'd heard about the stuff, but hadn't tried it. I asked Tommy if I could sample a can of the Brisk Iced Tea he was putting away.

"That stuff any good?" I asked him.

"Nah, I drink it 'cause it's terrible!" he told me, before reminding me, "the only good tea is sweet."

I confirmed that was a yes from Tommy and sampled a cold one. I can be a bit of a salad dodger when it comes to fried and carbohydrate-packed foods, but I struggle with many of the sweeter beverages of this world. That Brisk Iced Tea was good. I made a mental note to myself *not* to buy a pack so I didn't end up necking too much of it. If I could've, I would've. However, I would later become a fiend for Diet Mountain Dew.

Not having learned my lesson the first time in Minnesota, I thought I was up to being a good ol' Texan farm worker and chewing some tobacco. The stuff I had in mind this time was the stuff you actually chewed. It's a different kettle of fish from the tobacco you wedge in between your gum and lip. I wasn't going to make a habit of it. But coming to the United States, working as a tractor operator and not chewing tobacco seemed like a missed opportunity. I asked the crew to help me out.

I was promptly tossed a sample. The reaction from the seasoned chewers and dippers we had in the crew led me to believe that handing me the stuff they did was the equivalent to supplying a fifteen-year-old, who hadn't really drunk before, with a triple-shot of bourbon and a splash of soda pop at one in the afternoon on a Tuesday before gym class. Their warning was: Do *NOT* swallow it, whatever you do. The handy part for me in all this? I was about to head out for my nightly walk. I put a bit of wheat straw in the edge of my mouth, which did not stay there long, and headed off down the road.

Not wanting to waste the opportunity, I chewed as I'd been advised to and tried to let it relax me as it should. I created an imaginary scene. I pictured I was rolling along in a John Deere combine cutting some wheat, wearing a John Deere cap, listening to Sublime on the radio, and looking over at my diesel-powered Jeep Grand Cherokee that was parked at the edge of the field. It was a pleasant scene. But the image didn't last. Barely 300 feet into the walk, I had to spit it all out. It took me everything I had not to vomit all over the side of the road. From then on, I decided to stick to chewing sunflower seeds.

When it was sunny again, we headed up to the Helena lot to wash our combines and tractors. The drivers lined our gear up in a convoy, facing into the wash bay. The arrangement looked awesome. To this day I regret not taking a photo of it, although I think I'd left my phone back at camp when I heard we'd be on the water blasters that afternoon. We got busy greasing and fuelling up the machines so they were ready to go when the fields were right. The nearby area in the lot smelled like bovine manure. It was filled with weathered Peterbilt 379s, all marked with their family-owned ranch logos.

Out on the road next to the yard, I saw a military serviceman in the middle of a training run. Given the yard's proximity to Sheppard, my guess was that I was looking at an airman. Complete with the illuminous PT belt, he was trudging along next to the railway tracks. He was tiring fast and gradually moving slower and slower. He looked exhausted; he was probably stressed, and he was certainly lacking in electrolytes. It was hellishly hot that day. It was super humid. I still remember looking over and watching him slog his guts out just to keep moving.

Back at camp, with the grain still not ready, George called the crew truck drivers to attention. He was going to take them, in convoy, around Wichita Falls to show them where the grain elevator was. A grain elevator is a silo/storage facility where the trucks drop off the grain, beans, or seed they've been loaded with in the field. With no duties at that time for the field crew (the tractor and combine operators, which included me), I asked if I could ride along. I rode shotgun with Devin.

Wichita Falls was never a place that struck me as particularly Texan. I saw it as a city built to house those working on the adjacent military base or in one of the several agricultural or manufacturing-connected industries in the area. The air base housing stretched on for quite a while. It was clear there was always quite a bit going on in there. On our drive around I saw Jack In The Box, Carl's Jr., and Whataburger—food outlets I didn't remember seeing further north. There was also an abandoned joint called Big Momma's House. Judging by the width of the doors, the name didn't lie.

A short while later, the next member of our crew arrived. He was Jake, a straightforward, agreeable young man from northern Kansas, only a stone's throw from where we would later work. Jake was a licensed truck driver and an experienced farmhand who had a fall harvest under his belt. He'd run a grain cart. I made a mental note to ask him for advice, which I later did many a time. The only problem was, we already had a Jake on the crew (Jake from Tennessee). Tennessee Jake is an unforgettable person. Once you have met Tennessee Jake, you can never un-meet Tennessee Jake. To avoid confusion, the new team man would be referred to on the two-way radio as Helmer (his surname). Soon later, we added Philipp to the team. Another member for the 'Club International' section of the crew, Philipp had traveled all the way from Austria to get stuck into the Great North American Harvest.

Back at camp, I joined John to check over truck tires. While much of the field machinery was down the road at Helena, the grain-carrying trucks stayed with us at the camp. John gave me a running commentary of how to spot defects, quickly check cat-eyes, and the other things to look for on the undersides of the Holland's Kenworth T800 truck units and hopper bottoms (semi-trailers that open and unload from the bottom, used for carrying grain, seeds, and beans). My interest in trucks was growing by the day. Like grain harvesting, trucks were not something I knew a lot about at that time. John filled me in on all the good things in the trucking world, beginning with Caterpillar and Cummins Diesel, the engines the Holland's trucks were running. To complete the 'big three' of truck power plants, John also gave me a run-down on the Detroit Diesel Corporation.

A crew supper outing was on the cards. We piled into the two cars, the Lincoln and the Impala, and headed out. We cruised through Iowa Park and into Wichita Falls to RibCrib. Living up to everything the name suggested, RibCrib served up a cutting board of delicious pork ribs and other carnivorous treats. Although most of us knew each other fairly well by that point, it was good to sit around, drink a beer or two and just have a chat in a relaxed, non-work

33

environment. For dessert, I ordered something that was half-way between a fancy milkshake and a 'slider'. With its added booze, it kicked like an about-town cocktail. They were so good that if the RibCrib staff had kept bringing them, I'd have kept drinking them until the floor looked inviting.

I woke up again to the sound of rain hammering down on the roof above me. In northern Texas, it rains hard and will wake even the heaviest of sleepers. It was good that nature had woken me up at 4:30 am because we were about to roll out of camp and head on down the trail. We were off to Vernon, TX, for a safety and education morning with MacDon, the company that built the headers that were fastened to the front of our combines. Sue had coffee ready for us in the cook trailer. We got caffeinated and headed out.

We gathered about an hour away at Vernon in the hall area of a rodeo arena. Looking around the room, it appeared most of the guys in there were barely old enough to legally purchase a beer in the United States. I remembered I'd been able to buy a beer within U.S. law for more than half a decade. Practically everyone in the room was wearing a t-shirt or a checked long-sleeve shirt, and I'd say over ninety percent of them had a cap on. The remainder opted for the Stetson-style cowboy hat, also worn in other parts of the United States by livestock farmers. There is nothing that screams "I am a custom harvest crew member" like a t-shirt and a machinery cap, with a wrench and knife on your belt.

The MacDon session was brief, to-the-point and informative. I sat there trying to take all on board that I could. I also took mental notes of the terminology they used in case I was quizzed on it later. The handout brochure included a piece on the Darling farm back in little old New Zealand. Down south near Timaru, those Kiwi farmers harvested a world-record barley yield in 2015.

34

They hauled in a whopping 13.8 tonnes per hectare. That is some serious crop.

The next day it was the same drill, except this time we headed north to Frederick, Oklahoma, for the annual harvest breakfast event. That morning I added non-dairy creamer, a tasty vanilla flavor, to my coffee. It instantly reminded me of the Third Eye Blind song, 'Non-Dairy Creamer'. Thinking of that aging Third Eye Blind track wasn't the only time that day when life reminded me I was a lot older than most of the boys in our crew. Oklahoma looked as if it had shared the same downpour as us. The fields had massive puddles and there wasn't a piece of machinery moving. It wasn't a pretty sight for the increasingly weary farmers who wanted to get moving. We took an odd-looking route to get on the correct highway section to our destination. It appeared to be slowly dragging us in the right direction. Tennessee Jake remarked, "We're taking the route to get from our elbow to our thumb." I laughed at this southern anachronism as I loosely understood what I thought Jake meant. That was not the only time in the season that a famous Jake-ism would make an appearance.

The Frederick, OK, venue was a rural convention center of sorts. It had a strict 'No Vaping' policy. We chuckled at that. There appeared to be only two set age groups: the barely-twenty machinery operators and the sixty-ish owner-operators. Twenty-seven-year-old me was somewhere out in the open. I had a few years on most of our crew. As the show got underway, the announcer said it would be a "multi-denominational service" and "both green folk and red folk are welcome". This friendly nod to the state's strong Christian and agricultural influence, and John Deere versus Case IH rivalry produced a good laugh from all present.

After the presentation indoors, two Case IH employees gave a walk-around session outside with a brand-new Case combine harvester, just like one of ours. I tagged along to try and soak up more knowledge and blend in with the group. Like the MacDon team, the Case IH personnel on duty that day really knew their stuff, took questions well, and carried themselves like farming folks who really did care. Better still, they gave me a free hat. That morning I purposely didn't wear one. I am rarely seen without a hat. The crew asked me why I wasn't wearing one. I told them that if I went to a machinery show without a cap, I'd leave with a new one. I proved the theory correct by way of one free hat from the guys outside, and another from a prize bag I won in a draw. More than half the guys in our crew hit it big with the prize draw too. Not bad for a room with at least 150 or so people. I think we all had a pretty good time at Frederick that morning.

On the way back south towards the Texas state line, we called in to a standard issue 'just off the highway' general store. The various signs and pamphlets inside called for state-wide initiatives to lower taxes, look out for farmers, and support the troops. I was more than happy to give my business to a store with values like that! I bought a pack of local beef jerky and tried some fried okra, something of a harvest crew delicacy. Sue cooked some for us later on. It was mighty good. The okra reminded me of a bell pepper, one of my favorite vegetables since I was a child.

Back in Texas it was dry on the ground. Up to Helena, it was on to the machines to calibrate. I had a small blast on my tractor in the yard. My machine combination was a Case IH 280 Magnum tractor pulling a Brent grain cart. All my previous tractor driving experience, which wasn't extensive, went right out the window. I froze up and felt like I was reversing an expensive European vehicle off a car carrier with a busted steering column. In the cab with me, Tony offered some useful pointers and helped move my attention away from Cassie. While I was backing my tractor into position next to the rear of the combines, Cassie was in plain sight. He was waving his arms around like one of those inflatable figures that fly outside car yards, doing his best he could to ensure I would whack into the $2 million or so of equipment only feet away to my left. He slapped my back afterward and offered me his hearty congratulations for maneuvering in straight. I gave him a playful jab in the ribs and laughed with him.

The next morning, following another session at the Helena yard on the tools, we headed off to the Museum of North Texas History in Wichita Falls. The museum featured all kinds of exhibits on the surrounding area, including an intricate, moving-part replica of an oil pumping mechanism. The rest of the museum featured numerous odds and ends that somehow fit together in a perfect way. On show were areas dedicated to the Vietnam War, World War II, and various other conflicts and military operations the United States had involved itself in. At the end of our stroll around, I placed a pin on Whanganui, my home town in New Zealand, which was visibly marked on the wall-sized map for visitors. The museum curator asked us to sign the visitor's book, possibly to ensure his grants kept coming in. I did so happily, and made a donation to what I thought was an excellent little museum. When I return to Wichita Falls one day I will certainly pay the gentleman and his museum another visit.

After more rain overnight we headed back out at Helena to fuel up machines and perform our final walk-around and maintenance checks. One machine's fuel tank didn't do a very good job at holding its diesel. A makeshift siphon process got underway. The nearest big Case IH joint in Dallas didn't have a spare fuel tank of that kind, so a replacement was promptly arranged to be shipped down from Missouri. The Case IH customer service was impressive. I was told that if a bit of its machinery, provided it was acquired under a particular deal and/or warranty, broke down in the field, a kitted out and qualified Case IH-employed diesel mechanic would be on the scene within the hour.

In my tractor cab, I took a minute to fiddle around with the head unit and find a good radio station. It was typically Texan as I went from station to station: country, country, pop, country, country. Just as I was about to quit for the time being, I hit a station playing 'Angels Fall' by Breaking Benjamin. 'A *real* rock station,' I thought. Perfect. The sitting around wasn't to last. The two-way came to life with chatter and we got the call to idle up and get ready to move. Things were about to get real.

John rode shotgun with me in the cab on the way to the field. 'Roading' the machines was a common sight in rural America. As the term implies, 'roading' refers to moving the combines and tractors down a public road or highway under their own steam, as opposed to hauling them in on the back of a semi-trailer. All I had to focus on was driving the thing correctly, as we had truck drivers leading and tailing us in the company-marked pickup trucks. The field was only a few miles away. We rolled in through the gate, turned our flashing beacon lights off, and got in position to start cutting that wheat.

Rob performed the test-cut: a quick, bite-sized chunk of the field to see what was what. A truck driver zipped out to his machine, Combine #6, with an old plastic coffee container, filled it with freshly-harvested wheat, and headed straight to the nearest elevator in a pickup truck to get an accurate moisture reading. Wet grain isn't much help to anyone, so there are limits on what will and will not be accepted at the elevator. This reading must've come back just under 13%. All combines were ordered to idle up and prepare to move out. This was it. Harvest 2016 was officially underway.

I rode in Tractor #2, Tony's tractor, to observe the first run. The experienced Tony maneuvered his machine in and out of position with ease, lining up next to each combine harvester without batting an eyelid. Rob and each of the six combine operators would get on the two-way and let Tony know who had what, and who was where. Combine #1 was, at first, operated by John from the Fargo-Moorhead area, Minnesota, and later by Philipp from Bad Radkersburg, Austria. Combine #2 was run by Kelvin from Oakey, Queensland. Combine #3 was operated by Clint from Covington, Indiana. At the controls of #4 was Helmer from Beloit, Kansas. Combine #5 was commandeered by Tommy, from Centerville, Tennessee. Combines numbered one to five were brand new Case IH 7240 Axial Flow models, fresh from the factory at Grand Island, Nebraska. The remaining machine, Combine #6, a Case IH 8240 Axial Flow model, was operated by the boss and business co-owner, Rob Holland, from Litchfield, Minnesota. It was confirmed. I would be one of two grain cart operators for the season. My machine was Tractor #1.

The job of the grain cart driver is straightforward. It is their responsibility to go and fetch the product from each combine on the move and take it to a waiting truck. The aim of the game is to ensure a combine never has to stop and avoids having to roll around with much more than three-quarters of its payload intact. Once a combine's bin hit three-quarters full, its flashing beacon lights come on. If you're driving by a field sometime and you see those lights flashing on a combine, it means it's starting to get pretty full, and there's probably a grain cart driver blasting towards it in a hurry! When a combine needed unloading, it would extend its auger, a big metal pipe that moved out to the left of the machine. The grain cart driver would then position the cart (the trailer behind the tractor) directly underneath the auger, which began unloading product from the combine while the two machines were rolling along.

We went at it until about 8 pm. Standard practice at the end of a day's cutting (harvesting) was to park the machines neatly in a row. Not only does this look cool, but it is also practical. One reason for this formation is so the fuel truck can drive along behind the combines to get them all full in the morning. To get it just right, the two tractors will be at one end of the row and will keep a slightly wider spacing between them. That was so the truck could move in at an angle on the tractor's left-hand side where the fuel cap is located, as opposed to on the rear of the machine, where the fuel inlet point is located on a combine harvester. Sue fed us nachos for supper that evening. They were to die for. Back at camp, I deleted a tallboy can of Bud Light while looking out toward the air base and into the nearby field. It was idyllic.

The next day, it was my turn to idle up and join in the fight. I said a quick prayer before heading out to join the other machines in the field. I felt I needed to. I was far more nervous than I should have been. It was like I'd forgotten how to operate the tractor properly. I *knew* that I knew how. My brain and my proven tractor ability was like a muscle in my arm that wouldn't let me lift a smaller dumbbell weight at the gym that it had allowed me to lift a hundred times. The first combine I unloaded was Rob's. To this day, I am thankful he didn't make me do it on the run. I'd have been testing out my health insurance coverage with a heart condition if we had done it moving.

Rob took off in another direction. There was no option left but to quickly learn to unload on the run. Stationary unloads were generally avoided, unless two or three combines would pull up and unload simultaneously. The old trucking saying "If the wheels aren't turning, you aren't earning" applies to harvesting, too. You have to keep it moving. When you're sat there, you're still burning diesel and clocking up engine hours. That all costs. When you're moving, there's still an immense cost involved, but you're making money.

Kelvin's machine was the first combine I unloaded on the run. I spent most of the time watching the edge of the header—the 35'-wide attachment on the front of the combine—making sure I didn't go right into the side of it. My wheels would've been several feet away but, as a newbie, I was having a hard time getting used to the fact I'd need to drive so close to another big bit of gear. The next unloads were John and Helmer, as I remember. Normally I would have recorded such details. However, that first day at the controls was so hectic, the several hours we worked seemed like two hours. We were out there a lot longer than that.

With my grain cart full, meaning the onboard scales read more than 54,000 lbs, it was time to make my way to one of our trucks in the field. I swung the machine around and pulled up alongside the truck. To unload the contents of a grain cart into a truck, you just had to pull up alongside, unfold the cart's auger, then get to work. I ran through the unload process aloud in the cab, edged forward, and engaged the PTO (power take-off) to set the auger in motion. At first, it went fine. The problem was, I hadn't switched my transmission back into the right gear when I'd made it to the back of the trailer. I thought I'd made the correct change with the thumb selector. Apparently not. I meant to edge back, but I ended up going in the opposite direction; I had the revs up fairly high. And, bam! I spilled a good couple of hundred pounds of grain straight on the ground. The moment I saw George and Devin leap in the air and wave their arms I knew something was wrong.

My only relief was that I quickly worked out what I'd done wrong, and how not to do that next time. I apologized to George and Devin. I told them I'd make myself useful with the shovel as soon as we had completed the section. Devin patted me on the back and said not to worry. George just said, "Don't worry about it, have another go!" I appreciated their kind words. But I still felt like a tool.

About an hour after the grain spill incident, Rob's machine proved a bit much for a wet spot at one end of the field. We got on the two-way and called for backup. It was Flipper to the rescue. Flipper, the farm foreman, was a Texan local who was so laid-back he was almost falling over. He rolled in with his Case Steiger 535 HD and got busy pulling out the bogged combine. While the recovery operation was underway, I jumped out of my cab and got busy with the shovel. I was still fit at that point, barely a month out of my rigorous New Zealand gym routine. I managed to toss all the offending grain back in the truck after about fifteen or twenty minutes. While I was pleased I got it done that quick in the humid Texan heat, I thought it was a bit of a worry that I was more accurate with the shovel than I was with the auger. I knew I had better go about changing that quickly.

A new day, a new field. We knocked over the wheat on one side of Interstate 44 and geared up to head to the other side. The new field was larger and had a different feel to it. I was a day or two into operating my new tractor. I felt a little more comfortable. I was nowhere near 'at ease', but I was able to focus more on where to have the machine rather than being concerned about which control did what. A negative for that new field was its rougher section. We ended up calling that part 'The Baja Trail'. The badger holes in the rough patch, or whatever they were, made life very unpleasant if you drove over them at speed. The wheat yielded well. And, in that field, the cart operators always knew when a truck was coming. The engine brakes would sound off, loudly and proudly, as the trucks moved off the Interstate to the approach in the field.

The field went by without incident—right until a stroke of bad luck got Tony bogged. Tony's only crime was that he happened to drive through a bad spot only feet from where I had just made it through. The stubble was long, and the ground all looked the same. If you hit a soft patch, you'd only know about it when it was all too late. Fate, not lack of observation, got you bogged in that field. On that occasion, Tony and I were about to pass each other going in opposite directions. I was fully loaded.

Suddenly, I heard my engine revs change. I felt the back of my machine begin to pull away to one side. Without hesitation, I banged the multi-function handle forward to increase ground speed, and I straightened out. I owed that reaction to my background riding dirt bikes in the often muddy New Zealand conditions. I only *just* made it out, barfing out a thick cloud of diesel fumes in the process. Tony, who'd probably just seen what I had to do, appeared to hit the slightly wetter patch, only too late. Tony only had one combine's worth of wheat on board. If I'd driven where he did, I would have gone a story down.

As we got into a rhythm, we got quicker at moving from place to place. That afternoon we upped sticks and moved down a dead-end country backroad to the new field. It was a lot bigger than the rest. A job for a day or two, at least. After we got to work, I got some running pointers on how to fade into the unload position. As I would head straight for a combine, I'd get about in line with it and perform a gentle hairpin turn so I'd be in on its left-hand side ready to unload. It was good for general efficiency and it minimized the time the poor, overworked engine would have to spend sucking in the wheat dust that hung around constantly. Helmer flicked me some handy hints on the quiet, and, with that, my fades improved. He knew what to look for. I listened.

Another day, another go at it. The heat was searing and the mosquitos were treating us like a Walmart special. The big word was the DoT (Department of Transport) was out on the move and ready to pounce. Even if you did things by the book, it was a reminder to make sure you'd crossed your T's and dotted your I's. The DoT wasn't the only thing closing in on us; dark clouds began to form all around the field. From them shot some mean-looking lightning bolts. That damn weather, again, was about to make things more difficult for us.

Barely another day of cutting passed before the weather shut us down. After a trip out to the field to unload and haul out the wheat we still had on board from the previous night, we rallied back at camp. I suggested a few of us go out and fetch long-sleeve shirts to ward off the band of mosquitoes that would definitely be back when the rain cleared. I had a few takers. We drove to a nearby strip mall behind Sheppard AFB and found Sarge's Military Supply. I bought myself a current pattern Air Force long-sleeved top, a Marine Corps woodland digital camouflage long-sleeved top, and a 1990s-era woodland camouflage long-sleeved top. Not a bad haul for about $40 all up.

On the way back around the front of the air base, near the aptly-named Missile Road, we saw a B-52 bomber. It was parked right on there on the tarmac. I stared at it out the window in awe. Its distinctive wing pattern and ageless frame jumped right out at me. I'd seen the B-52 on documentaries, in films, and on TV. Since I was a child, I'd known what it looked like, thanks to my maternal grandfather's stint as a pilot. Although I don't believe he ever flew a B-52, Grandad did show me what scores of different aircraft looked like. I never thought I'd ever get that close to one. The others in the car questioned why I was staring at that military airplane as if I'd just discovered fire.

With some more spare time, a few of us headed into Wichita Falls. First stop: a gun store. I walked the aisles with Kelvin and held a variety of shotguns, rifles, sub-machine gun-style firearms, a local AK-47 variant, and more. I got talking to the store attendant about gun laws in Texas versus New Zealand and firearms regulations in general. The attendant had a pistol holstered on his waist, presumably with a round chambered. I asked him the question I really wanted to ask. He answered. Yes, there had been incidents of folks who had come in and attempted to rob a gun store, in Texas, at gunpoint, he confirmed. I guess the Darwin Awards still exist for a reason.

Come morning, it was hosing down—just for a change. After breakfast and a good session reading *Clear and Present Danger*, I found out George was doing a parts and equipment run across the state line to Altus, Oklahoma. George kindly let me come along for the ride, along with a couple of others. Across in Oklahoma, the landscape flattened out. There was more green and yellow machinery. The Texans, at least around Wichita Falls, tended to run red machinery instead of green. Sadly, no machine in sight was moving. There was water on the deck everywhere. That day, local harvesting was deader than a Texas salad bar. We linked up with the Case IH service guys and collected the parts we needed.

Back in the Lone Star State, we headed out to the Helena yard to load combines and tractors for road transport. We were about done and preparing to head back to camp for lunch when I noticed George standing idly and looking into the sky. He was turned away from the group, facing east, staring in the general direction of where we'd gotten soaked on the machines a few days earlier. A big, ominous black cloud crept closer and closer. The sky above us was a darker shade of grey, but to my eye, it didn't look too threatening. I walked over to George, looked where he was looking, and turned to look

45

at him. George spun around and said, "Boys, let's get under cover. We are about to get wet!" Within about ten seconds, the heavens opened and absolutely plowed us. It was like George had a sixth sense to know the weather was about to empty an entire magazine. Fortunately, all of us had something to climb in or underneath.

A day later, the order was given to shift half the machinery to Farmers Valley, TX. Tony's cart was headed out with three other combines. The entire crew rallied at the Farmers Valley property so we could quickly unload the gear and assist a fellow Midwest crew, Brown Harvesting, who were working nearby. They ran John Deere, so it was no surprise to find out they were a good bunch of guys. I wound up on supper-run duty, so I ferried Sue's ready-made field meals from camp back out to the machines. Quote of the day went to George. On the way in, passing through Vernon, he said: "I like this place already. It has a Braum's." There was no argument from me on that one.

On the way back to camp that night, Helmer asked if I knew about 'Ten Rounds with Jose Cuervo'. Bemused, I told Helmer that to my knowledge, no, I had not consumed a raft of alcoholic beverages with a person of that name. Jake, John, Helmer, and Clint burst out laughing. Genuinely confused, I wondered what I'd just walked into. I threw up my hands and looked around the other faces in the car for clues. Helmer advised me it was a song, pulled it up on his phone and played it loud for everyone to hear. The tequila jokes came thick and fast.

Clint: "Do you know the rhyme about tequila?"

Me: "No … "

Clint: "One tequila, two tequila, three tequila, floor! Know what happens after five tequilas?"

Me: "No, what happens?"

Clint: "Yeah, no-one knows."

The Texas adventure was not to last much longer. The crew would temporarily split. Five of us had orders to move two states north. We were off to Kansas with George. Following an 0500 get-up to load machinery and make final preparations, I found myself working as a roofer that afternoon up on top of the cook trailer to seal up a few holes. It sure was warm up there. But it offered a front-seat view of an ongoing military aerial exercise involving several Black Hawk helicopters. Although our Australian neighbours do, New Zealand's military does not run Black Hawk helicopters. The opportunity to watch one hover up close was something I counted myself lucky to see. And, as usual, the nearby jets were winging their way around a few miles away, regularly zipping over towards our campsite, where I worked on the roof.

Kingman, Kansas

Kingman, KS, is legendary in the world of Holland Harvesting. Before you went there, you heard a lot about it. The days were long and the nights were hot, you were told. If you looked up Holland Harvesting on YouTube, you would see copious references to, and images from, Kingman. On the road south to Texas, a point would be made that you were in line with and/or close to Kingman. Some might say that if you were involved with Holland Harvesting and you didn't hear all about, and experience Kingman, KS, then you weren't really there! When my double-set alarm woke me up early that June morning in Texas, I was excited to be heading off to Kingman to finally check it out for myself. Although work-wise it was intermittent and hard-going for all concerned, I enjoyed Texas. The culture, the people, the geography—it all left a lasting impression on me. But we had a job to do. It was time to head north and do the business two states up.

I took a seat next to Clint in vehicle #17, one of the Holland's two Dodge Ram 2500, Cummins-powered pickups. We would be hauling a tow-behind Cherokee trailer unit that housed our foremen, Cory and George. Just over the border in Oklahoma, we pulled into a Love's

Travel Stop to fetch some breakfast. As mentioned, an opportunity to get some food with an uncertain day ahead was an opportunity best taken with both hands. One thing Love's did particularly well was its selection of coffee on tap. If there was a variety you could think of, I'm sure it was there right in front of me that morning.

I picked the strongest, meanest-sounding variety of freshly brewed coffee from some equatorial nation, probably mixed with a bit of taurine and gunpowder. I added some fresh milk with a dash of vanilla creamer. I have been a coffee drinker for a long time; a gas station or truck stop coffee was something I considered a real treat on Harvest 2016, but there wasn't always a chance to grab one. Whenever I could, I did. Sue always ensured we always had enough coffee at breakfast to blow out a kidney, so the supply and availability of coffee wasn't the issue. The on-tap selection at places like Love's never ceased as a novelty for me. Around $1.50 bought a large, American-sized coffee. I was sold.

The trip north through the remainder of Oklahoma and into Kansas was pretty cruisy. We called into a gas station just north of the state line. The buildings around it were whitewashed and run-down. It was just like a setting from an old-school crime film. The place had a *Reservoir Dogs* feel about it. The gas station yard was full of Peterbilt 379s. They were parked, showroom style, all in a row. Clint asked that I remain calm, keep myself composed, and promise to come back to the pickup one day if I walked over and had a look at them. I already had my coffee, so I didn't need anything from the gas station. All there was to do was wander off and gawk at the Peterbilts like an overgrown child.

As we pulled out of the gas station I got a phone call from George. He asked how we were getting on with our travels. I told him we were rolling along just fine and we'd made it to Kansas.

George paused and asked me, "Whereabouts in Kansas are ya?"

I paused and looked around for some kind of landmark. I temporarily forgot I was a long way from the mountainous, hill-covered, rough geography I'd grown up in back home where there's always a lake, a river, a hill, or a gorge to remind you where you are. I was about to tell George, "Uh, well, um, it's dead flat and there's elevators and combines everywhere." There was a small problem with that. My description would have covered much of the state of Kansas which, area-wise, had more than three-quarters of the land mass of my entire home country. "We're just over the state line, George, we're headed for camp, we'll get there as soon as we can," I replied.

If there was a mental picture in my head of what real American wheat country looked like, Kingman was exactly it. With its red brick roads, old buildings, and flat, beautiful farmland, the town was a perfect caricature of the American Midwest I'd heard so much about. To top it off, it was blazing hot. There wasn't a cloud in the sky. Located in the county of the same name, Kingman is about fifty miles north of the Kansas–Oklahoma state line and home to a population of around 3,000. But it was June. Harvest time. The custom cutters were rolling in from the south by the day.

The first Kansas job was to set up George and Cory's trailer, which we'd hauled north. At the farm headquarters, a few miles out of Kingman, we hooked the trailer facilities and ensured it was good to go. The cook trailer—where we ate many of our meals, and also where Devin, Cassie, and Tony slept—would be parked up next to George and Cory's trailer when the remainder of the crew traveled north a couple of days later. There was no rest for the wicked. We got the word and headed straight out to the field to get into it. Little did I know, we were about to hit some canola.

The field was a sprawling, tan-colored expanse. Instead of the usual soft, low-lying wheat stubble, it had the taller, spindly canola stubble all through it. The canola crop had been recently swathed, ready for us to pick up. In place of the 35-foot-wide header on the front of the combines, they were fitted out with canola pickup headers. A simpler and smaller implement, these headers were about twelve feet wide. They had rubber centers with small, plastic hooks fitted to grab hold of the crop. The combines lowered their headers a few inches off the ground, drove straight over the stuff, and took it right into the machine. It was simple but dusty work.

The Kansas Canola Crew sprung into action. Kelvin, Clint, and John steered their combines around the field while Jake and George ensured the trucking side of the operation kept rolling. I was in the middle of the two groups, moving the tractor around the best I could. In the few hours the day before I got there, Tennessee Jake had driven my tractor. That, right there, explained why my radio was tuned into a country music station. I hit the seek dial once to see what would happen. Immediately, it found a station playing 'Blue on Black' by Kenny Wayne Shepherd. That told me it could still be a country or blues station. I love that song, so I left it playing. After Mr Shepherd finished up, the station segued into 'Far Behind' by Candlebox. An outstanding choice. Following that, I learned the resident DJ on the station, Hank the Mechanic, was into playing hard rock music from the 1960s to the present day for custom harvesters working the fields. In Kingman, I never went near the seek button on the radio again. The T95 station rocked.

There was canola in the fields that surrounded us and it was all ours. Looking after three combines still kept me out of trouble, but it wasn't as intense as charging around after six of them at once. One thing about working canola was the headers on the front of the combines weren't nearly as wide. Although you still needed to be mighty careful and watch what you were doing, you had virtually no chance of whacking into a canola header with your tractor. Another thing about swathed canola was its dust. The crop was out of the ground, devoid of life and moisture. That made for a dry, rough combination that clogged radiators, cab air cooling systems and, at times, made it mighty difficult to see what was what, particularly at night. That evening we trucked on until about 11 pm when George brought us some McDonald's. It really hit the spot. Then he announced we'd be holed up in a motel that evening. I slept for the entire seven hours we were allowed. It felt like I barely shut my eyes.

The next morning we continued right where we left off. The constant sun and the slight breeze must've dried out any overnight moisture left behind. We barely had to wait before getting straight into it. Some of the swaths were a bit rough. Judging by the deep trenches on the ground where it looked like the operator had managed to get themselves stuck several times, we guessed they must've done it pretty tough trying to windrow all that canola on time. Although Jake and George had a bit of a trek to get to the elevator, I never had to wait for them in the field when I was fully loaded. Just like the area we worked in Texas, there wasn't any problem with switching on the engine brake on the way in. If George or Jake were about to hit the field, I heard them well before I saw them. Jake and George typically weren't shy about using their trucks' engine brakes on full noise.

That day, the combines did not stop unless they had to un-clog and reverse a header. Because of the awkward approach (the field entry and exit point) angle in one particular field, I had to creep out through a gate and onto a public road to load the trucks. It made me a little nervous the first time. Then I stopped and thought about it for a second. I was way heavier than any pickup I might run into, even if it was a decked-out, Cummins-powered Dodge Ram 3500. The only trucks I had seen so far were ours, and any other semi-truck driver would have easily seen me from a quarter mile away. The narrow opening at the gate didn't make things easy. It proved to be a real confidence booster. Kelvin managed to snap a photo of me loading on that road. I have it proudly displayed to this day.

T95, as expected, was in top form that afternoon. I liked its catering for different generations: 1960s and 1970s-era fans got The Doors and Pink Floyd. Children of the 1980s were treated to Guns N' Roses and Metallica; 1990s products heard Nirvana, Fuel, and The Offspring. The 2000s to present-era fan base got Staind, Puddle of Mudd, and a new track called 'Emotionless' by Red Sun Rising. That song would later become something of a Kansas staple for us.

After we parked up and idled down that night, we headed to our new campsite. Our trailer was situated behind a farmer's shed near a main county road. It was quiet, out of the way and not too far from town. The only downer was that for some reason, I got no mobile reception. There was, however, a shed full of Chevrolet Corvettes right next to our trailer. I counted at least four when I peered in the window. The word was that we weren't allowed in there for a look around. 'Oh, we'll see about that,' I thought to myself.

When we'd finished off the last of the canola the next morning we got orders to prepare the combines and tractors for roading. The mission was to drive back to the farm headquarters where we'd set up George and Cory's trailer a few days earlier. Kelvin pointed out, correctly, that we were about to set in for a bit of a drive to get out there. After we left the field we drove past a fish farm. I did a double-take to make sure I wasn't seeing things. A fish farm was not something I'd imagined I'd see in heartland Kansas, but there you go!

The air temperature felt like it had reached steakhouse kitchen levels by the time we made it to the farm headquarters. My phone, which worked there, said it was just over ninety. It felt hotter than that. Before we hit the nearby wheat, which there was a lot of, we got a chance to grease and clean up our machinery. My cab air filter and radiator looked like a pair of lungs from an aging rock star when I blew them out with the air compressor. The first wheat cut in Kansas would be performed by the three wheat-ready combines that had just come up from Texas. That meant I would be the runner for the day.

As the runner, I would stand by in the pickup ready to fetch any parts, supplies, or articles needed for Tony and the three combines harvesting the wheat. That evening, back home, it was first test (international) match of the year for the All Blacks, New Zealand's national rugby team. It is always one of the bigger events in the Kiwi sporting calendar. That was the first opening night of test match rugby I had missed in more than twenty years. Although I enjoyed settling into Kansas and getting amongst it with the crew, I did feel a little homesick that afternoon.

It was a bright and early start to work the next morning. Only a portion of the farmer's wheat was ready to be cut. The rest certainly wasn't far off. Rob opted to run three combines and one tractor that day. I was drafted to pilot vehicle duty. Still a tad nervous about driving on what was, for me, the wrong side of the road, I gladly accepted my assignment and connected up the pickup's flashing beacon. The lead pilot vehicle would typically stay at least a quarter mile ahead of the road-going machines. The pilot driver's job was to ensure other motorists were aware some big machinery was heading towards them, as well as to communicate to the crew on the two-way radio what traffic was coming down the road towards them.

When you move out of a cambered country road onto a highway in a bit of farm machinery, it isn't always easy to see what's going on down the trail.

Rob's bright red Dodge Ram 2500 Laramie was a pleasure to drive. It was badass. And it came complete with a button-activated exhaust brake, a quieter variant of the louder engine brake setup you would find on a semi-truck tractor unit. Still new to the trade of operating larger farm machinery, my general knowledge of it all wasn't even close to the rest of the crew's. One thing I did bring to the party was sharp communication skills and a straightforward, usually mature demeanor. I think Rob, Cory, and George knew that with me up front in the pilot role they were always going to get a clear and present picture over the radio of what was going on up ahead. And, should a situation arise, I could play the diplomat if required.

That day, like the day before, was sizzling. There wasn't any trouble with moisture. Rob and the team made short work of the available wheat. During the truck drivers' travels to and from the elevator that day, which happened to be smack bang in the middle of town, word traveled fast that there were some pretty girls at the local swimming pool. When the late morning turned into afternoon, someone queried on the two-way if that particular crowd was still occupying the pool complex. Cassie told us all he would "Go extra slowly and check".

"What were you doing at the pool there, Cassie?" Rob asked on the two-way, wryly. He knew exactly what was going on—it wasn't lost on him. He was our age once.

"Ahhh, just making sure everything was good and ok, Mr Holland," Cassie confirmed.

In Kingman, the truck drivers had to move across an intersection (West & East Sherman Avenue and North & South Main Street) and reverse back over it in order to properly maneuver into the elevator portal to unload. It wasn't a move for the faint-hearted. A truck driver who successfully completed the process would cop an eyeful of the pool on the way out back to the field. Cassie did the right thing. He had carefully assessed the environment surrounding him from every direction, including any attention-grabbing sights on either side of the road.

Back on pilot duty that afternoon I was out, up ahead, in the pickup. We'd moved on from the field and tracked back the way we came without incident. I had just turned off the highway onto the road which led straight down to the farm headquarters. About two hundred yards out, I saw what I thought might have been an ATV crawling along in the middle of the road. I put the pedal to the metal and blasted down there. It was a local gentleman, creeping along on a tiny old John Deere lawn tractor, complete with a small green trailer.

I got out, said hello, asked him how he was doing, and told him he may want to pull his little green machine off to one side for a moment. He gently asked, "Why's that, sir?"

As if on cue, Rob rounded the corner in his combine, followed immediately by two others and a tractor. Again, briefly forgetting I wasn't back home, I jerked my thumb over my shoulder and said, "Uh, look behind you, bro."

The gentleman looked over his shoulder and, at the sight of the big, red juggernaut heading straight towards us, he proceeded to make his way off the side of the road.

Back at the farm headquarters, we performed any outstanding maintenance and service work that needed doing and temporarily pulled up. The active field crew had knocked over all the available wheat there was to cut. The weather wasn't any colder, and we had a few hours of free time. So what were we going to do? There was only one answer to that—head to the pool! Half of me wanted to catch up on a few emails and run errands. The other half of me that was sweaty, hot, covered in dust, and needed to blow off some steam told the email-inclined half of me to get stuffed. After a quick pit-stop at the local Dollar General to fetch swimming togs, we headed straight for the pool complex.

Both my parents are keen water dwellers, so I was fortunate to be raised in a household that valued water safety, as well as swimming for fitness and fun. Mum had me zipping around swimming pools from a young age. Growing up, I went for many a swim at the beach, in the river, and in the school pool. In middle school, I even won a couple of swimming events. Back in Wellington, New Zealand, I swam for fitness. Still, I hadn't been for a recreational dip at an outdoor pool for some time. We paid our entry fees, threw off our towels, and plunged into the deep blue.

We fooled around and engaged in general horseplay for a good hour or so in the afternoon heat. We got a quiet talking-to for doing flips into the pool. The lifeguards didn't want the younger generations breaking their necks as they copied our somersaults. But we were still free to engage in bombs, swan dives, and belly busters. After a day sweating in and out of machines in a wheat field, diving into the cool, fresh, blue water in the Kingman Swimming Pool that hot, June afternoon was a feeling of refreshment that was right up there.

The remaining wheat quickly readied itself for harvest, no doubt helped along by the perfect cutting weather. I hadn't tackled any wheat, or six combines at once, since Texas. I was anything but experienced as a grain cart operator, so it took an hour or two for the newly-formed rust to wear off. The new field wasn't the easiest, either. It was packed full of curves and awkward angles, as opposed to the more typical rectangular fields which consisted of long, straight runs. I'd barely come to the end of a loading maneuver and I'd have to stop, turn on myself and blast off after the next combine. T95 hummed away in the background, helping my day along with a bit of Dio and Guns N' Roses, plus 'Emotionless' by Red Sun Rising. It wasn't really a proper day of Kansas harvesting without that track. That day's work extended several hours into the night. I remember it well, because that night, I managed a real circus act.

Even in Kansas, a place crawling with custom harvesters all operating at once, we would usually be at least a quarter mile from the nearest machine that wasn't one of ours. At night, even with no field dividers or boundary markers of any sort, there was little to no chance of wading into someone else's harvesting operation. I'd never worked somewhere so flat and short of any big, natural landmarks. My beginner's nerves, my ability to lose my sense of direction on the flat countryside, and my inclination towards anything colored green and yellow was about to come to the boil.

It was about 10:30 at night. We'd entered a new field with an odd layout. It was divided in two by a block of trees. To get from one section to the other you had to make your way down a narrow trail which led through the trees. It was disorientating and it slowed things down. It was dark before we even saw the field, so our only impressions of it were formed by watching where everyone else's spotlights shone. I'd had a big day on my tractor. I was a bit stressed; I was tired. Rob asked me how many trucks I'd loaded. Us grain cart operators always kept a clipboard on our person with that information recorded. I told Rob I'd take a look. I grabbed my clipboard and tallied the numbers.

A few seconds earlier, Helmer had asked if I could come and collect his wheat. I'd told him, "Sure, all good." In the few seconds it took me to get the sum total and radio it to Rob, I lost my bearings a bit. I pushed the stick forward and headed straight for the combine.

Helmer popped back on the radio, "Paul …" he said. He paused and drew my name out.

I thought to myself, 'Easy on, Helmer, be with you in a second, bro.' As I coasted forward, for a second, I remember thinking something wasn't quite right. I brushed the thought aside as quickly as it came on and headed for the combine in front of me.

As I got a bit closer, the combine turned around and headed off at a right angle. During the turn, the operator slowly craned his neck around and stared. His facial expression was fixed somewhere between bewilderment and downright amusement. The problem was, that combine operator and Helmer were not the same person. Worse, that combine had a logo with an image of a deer, and it was green and yellow. Then, it hit me. I'd driven onto the next farmer's property and attempted to unload one of their combines. I said something unfit for print and quickly turned around. The other farmer's wheat was cut about the same height as ours, there were no field division markings, and this guy was cutting no more than a few hundred feet from us. Quietly, I wondered if anyone else had seen what I'd done. When I made it to Helmer and unloaded him, he looked across at me. The look on his face and his shaking head removed any doubt that my extracurricular move remained a secret.

It was humid and sticky the next morning. We had to wait up. I made the most of the break and cleaned my windows and cab interior. Over in another field, I saw the John Deere combine from last night doing its thing. I assume the same guy the previous night was in there again that morning. I bet he was there, listening to his country music station, in his own little world, and that he looked over at us and thought to himself, 'Which one of those Case IH-running boys was the simpleton who tried to come and unload me last night?'

The word on our two-way and in the local weather reports was that a big storm was coming. Nothing too serious, but enough to stop a day's harvesting if Mother Nature clenched her fists. We carried on undeterred, ready to deal with the storm when or if it turned up. The first job that day was roading out, back through Kingman, to a new area several miles away. That drive would take us past the pool. But we'd had our fun there for the time being. I enjoyed the drive through central Kingman. Not many people got to drive down the main street of an American farming town, with their friends, in half-million-dollar pieces of equipment and have everyone give way as if you were a presidential motorcade. To some, that might not seem exciting. But for us boys who'd come from around the world and across the United States to do it, it was fun. The memorable part of that morning began just after we'd made a right turn from North Main Street onto East D Avenue.

Every piece of Holland Harvesting equipment was equipped with a two-way radio setup. Right from the cook trailer to every truck, tractor, and combine. It was always possible that another crew using similar equipment would inadvertently creep onto the same channel as us. As far as I knew, it only happened twice on our harvest. This time in Kingman was one of the funnier moments of Harvest 2016.

We had passed through the intersection. As we were about in line with Smitty's Carry Out on East D Avenue—where we would later go for a delicious off-day lunch—my two-way lit up. The audio quality wasn't the best, as another crew's radio traffic was walking over the top of ours. The story went something like this: Another crew had been hard at work earlier that morning and it'd had a couple of mishaps with tires. The crew was under the pump, working against the clock, and not in a position to be able to replace the tires in a hurry.

"That tire was so worn you could see the air on it!" one voice said, in a strong, almost comical southern accent.

The other, with a similar accent, shot back: "Well y'all busted two of them already today, and I can't afford another one of them sum'bitches!"

The rest of the exchange consisted of a similarly-toned back-and-forth that was only just audible. What a scream. I laughed my ass off in my tractor cab as I listened to the gripping rural drama unfold over the airwaves. For a moment, I believed it was Tennessee Jake having a laugh on the radio. It turned out Clint and Helmer heard the exchange too. Helmer said that he too thought it sounded like Tennessee Jake. Later on, I ran the ordeal past Jake. He laughed as I recounted the conversation to him, and he approved of it. He confirmed that, no, it wasn't him.

We pushed beyond the city limits of Kingman and headed to the east. The fields seemed to get bigger and bigger. They looked ripe for long rows and minimal hassles. During part of the journey, we had to cross over a bridge above U.S. Route 400. We had pilot vehicles up front and in pursuit as we crossed in single file. I won't forget rolling above that six-lane highway all the way up there in my tractor cab, which was a good seven-plus feet off the ground. I could see a mile in every direction. It was a perfect opportunity to observe the upcoming fields and what they had in store.

As a grain cart operator, I always looked out for anything in the field that might impede what I was going to do and/or serve as a landmark. I might need to help direct a truck driver to a new area or give Tony a description of where another combine was. It was always good to have something to work with—for example, a block of trees, an oil pumpjack, a field division, and so on. There wasn't anything like that in these new fields. They were nothing but sprawling expanses of Kansas wheat. We spent the next couple of days going at it in those long fields near the highway. The wheat was damn good. We must've gone alright, because there was an airborne drone overhead that kept a beady eye on us.

The new area's harvest continued productively. We had a good rhythm going. The combines pretty much never had to stop. The rows were long and easy. Us grain cart boys never had to wait for a truck to roll into the field. It is an awkward place to be as a grain cart operator, in the field loaded with 52,000 lbs of grain and nowhere to put it. The combines stop. Then, everything becomes your fault all of a sudden. Also, it is anything but easy being a harvest trucker. They can get held up or caught out for a variety of reasons out there on the highway. Sure, the grain carts go and fetch the payload from the combines, but if there's nowhere for us to put it, things go pear-shaped very quickly. People stress the importance of grain cart operators. I would say to them: 'Sure, but if you're a grain cart operator and there's no truck ready to be loaded, you are an uncomfortable grain cart operator'. Our truck drivers did a stellar job, especially in Kingman, KS. As a grain cart guy, I could not have done without them for a moment. Without Devin, Cassie, Jake, John, Cory, and George in our Cummins and Cat-powered 18-wheelers, Tony and I would've gone nowhere fast.

The talk going around that night was that the local elevator was absolutely humming. A generous chunk of that freshly harvested wheat came from Holland Harvesting trucks. The gross domestic product of the State of Kansas had a few dollars added to it that June evening—right until the storm began to close in. The verdict on the two-way was concise: park up, idle down and tarp up—*quick!*

As we were parking up and idling down, Helmer, our resident Kansas local, showed me a better angle at which to park my tractor. I hesitated for a moment. Then I thought I probably shouldn't second-guess a man who'd spent his whole life in a place I'd been in for under a fortnight. I dove back in, moved the tractor, and tarped up. I bent my grain cart tarpaulin pole in the process, thanks to the wind racing by. At no point were we in any sort of danger. But with limited visibility, sand flying everywhere, sleeting that had set in, and some thunder and lightning to complement the rapid wind gust tearing through, there was no question we were close to the business end of the storm. It was a small pocket of Midwestern chaos. Kelvin climbed up on his combine, took a few good snaps, and formed a Titanic pose, at my suggestion. We piled into the vehicles and got the hell out of Dodge.

Following a sleep-in and another road trip back through Kingman, we went at it again on the opposite side of town near some irrigated wheat. That field was memorable because I almost wore an irrigator setup around my machine. Every operator has done it at least once. That turn where, as soon as you make it, you realise you've overplayed your hand, but it's too late to pull out. That day, it was me. In the new field, I made a hairpin turn near the irrigator, fully loaded. I knew the irrigator was there. I'd kept my eye on it the whole time. I pulled right back on the stick to slow the turn, purely out of caution. It paid off.

About three-quarters of the way through the turn, I knew I'd flown too close to the sun. I tightened up as much as I could. It wasn't enough. There was no way I could reverse out. It looked like only an oxygen-acetylene torch or some sneaky maneuvering could save me. The oxy torch wasn't anywhere nearby, and striking it up in the field probably wasn't a very good idea. As I crept closer, my side mirror touched the solid metal of the irrigator when I came to a stop. The easy fix? Quickly jump out of the cab, unscrew the side mirror's fastening, pull it back, inch forward, and get on with life.

I leapt out of the cab and did that as quickly as I could. Right as I climbed back in and switched the transmission back into gear, I saw Rob's combine, facing me, about 150 feet away. It would've been next to impossible for him not to have seen what I'd just done. I expected, any second, to cop a blast from Rob about being careful and not smacking his brand-new tractor into one of the local farmer's irrigator setups. The expected *Paul, what the hell! Paul, keep that damn tractor away from the irrigator there, boy!* over the radio was replaced with silence. Rob never said anything to me about it later. Either he was on the phone and somehow wasn't looking at the moment of truth, or he did see, and observed that I'd realised my sin and slowed his tractor down that much that I didn't wreck anything. I will never know whether or not Rob saw what I did. But I know I learned my lesson there and then—if it looks like you could be a wee bit close, keep away and make the damn turn someplace else!

In the new area we moved to, when I wasn't attempting to shunt irrigators, I ogled a brand new John Deere 9570RX. It was articulated and had not two tracks but four. Case IH had been in the quad track game for a while, so the 9570RX was John Deere's answer to the newly emerging market for these high-powered tractors. Loaded with a Cummins 14.9 liter QSX15 engine, it was rated at 570 horsepower. If you wanted one, you'd need to part way with around half a million U.S. dollars. Earlier, we'd spotted the 9570RX back at farm headquarters where everyone took photos, regardless of whether they were Team Case or Team Deere. And there it was. All on its own, sat next to a block of trees, ready to work the field. We learned it was part of a demonstration exercise the farmer was running. I think everyone on the crew that day worked on their own lines for the farmer to convince him, should an off day arise for us, that they should be the one to hop in the cab for a test run. I did. I would've told him that as the designated John Deere-mad tractor operator and former John Deere dealership employee, it should be me up there in that cab. No doubt about it!

A flat-out, hassle-free couple of days went by. Most of the wheat was irrigated. It was thick and heavy. We burned a lot of diesel. In those sections, the farmer's operation moved as fast as we did. We would harvest a field and, before we were even out of there, the farmer's two John Deere 9470Rs roared into life and started dragging harrows. One field, which happened to be right next to the elevator we were using, was round. That was a new one for me. The practice of loading and unloading wasn't all that different at all to the other fields, but operating within a big circle just seemed a little odd. It would've been a bonus for the trucking boys. They had a trip of approximately 2,000 feet to the queue for the elevator.

Come about 3 pm, we were done with Kingman. We idled down, parked up, and brought over one of the tandem trucks with the big air compressor. It was time for the job we loved to hate: blowing off combines. That hot, exhausting work was something that needed to be performed before moving upstate or across any border. You didn't do yourself any favors by taking to the highway with machinery that looked dusty and neglected. The entire process involved blowing off all combines and headers with an air compressor-powered nozzle before loading them onto the purpose-built semi-trailers for road transport. That afternoon would have been close to 100 degrees. A few crew members had to sit down and take a breather with a swig of Gatorade. It was a day when, if you weren't properly hydrated, you were a prime candidate for a bout of heat stroke. Sue brought us a delicious beef supper to end the day, which we ate sprawled across the various farm implements in the shed. I perched myself on the steps of a self-propelled John Deere spray rig to tuck in.

The morning after I'd heard 'November Rain' by Guns N' Roses on T95, we woke up to a legitimate Kansas downpour. After the trip to the farm headquarters for breakfast, which was our daily routine, we found out we had the day off. Although we were loaded and ready to move upstate, hydroplaning, busy highways, and heavy, oversized loads was not a combination to be tested out. I headed off with John, Helmer, and Jake to get a haircut. The man in the local barbershop, who had the high school football team's logo on the window, appeared to know every cattle rancher, farmhand, and custom cutter at that end of the state. There are many just like him at home—the barber who, way back when, played a few rep rugby games for the local side, countless senior club matches, and knew which schoolboy 1st XV member could and could not tackle, kick, run and pass effectively. Like his New Zealand equivalents, he offered great conversation. He gave me a fresh high-and-tight haircut at a small-town price. I have routinely worn a haircut in that style ever since.

As we pulled back into the trailer area where we were staying, the owner of the property came over to chat. He asked us to holler out if we needed anything, or if we wanted to have a look at his car collection. With that invitation, the two guys next to me walked straight through the door and into the shed. I dashed into our trailer, only feet away, and rounded up the other boys so they could join in too. The property owner, a former custom harvester himself who ran John Deere machinery and Peterbilt trucks, let us have free reign in the shed. We sat in, looked at, and took photos of his well-preserved Chevrolet Corvettes. The model range stretched back for more than forty years. Some were under covers. Others sat up on the hoist. The remainder sat with the bonnets facing out to the roller door, ready to tear up the open road and obliterate speed limits.

He pointed out one model he'd owned for sixteen years and had only put 4,000 miles on. He then climbed into it, fired it up, and revved the living daylights out of it. He encouraged us all to take photos and videos to send to our friends. It was clear he'd been in charge of young men for a long time. He understood them. He knew what made them tick. Instead of saying 'Hey, watch it, don't touch that' or 'Easy up on that, get out of there' and so-on, he let us wander amok knowing we'd respect the automobiles, be careful, and treat them with the reverence they deserved. At the end of the walk around, a few of us got to see his multi-wall display of full metal, die-cast John Deere machinery models. It was incredible. We were in the presence of a real, avid collector and enthusiast.

On a non-harvesting day, after breakfast, we'd typically be responsible for feeding ourselves. That was the deal we signed up to. A quick poll of the group confirmed no-one was in a food preparation kind of mood. We made tracks for town. Jake suggested we call into Smitty's Carry Out, the restaurant we passed during the infamous blown-tyre conversation on the two-way radio. Smitty's is an old-school burger joint that specializes in traditional hamburgers and onion rings. I ordered a fresh cook-up of just that. There are few, if any, menu items on God's Earth that I would have chosen over what Smitty's Carry Out had to offer me and my friends that day. It's still one of the tastiest meals I've ever eaten.

After we ordered up and took our seats, I found a copy of the local newspaper and got reading. The harvest report was detailed, filled with agricultural jargon, and quoted several farmers on their state of play. It was clear this paper was written for a local population that was mad about wheat farming. It was typical for a rural publication: laid-back with a real community feel. Also included was a jobs board and a recipe section, including a detailed step-by-step guide on how to prepare roasted skunk. When our food came, I stowed the paper away to read, literally, on a rainy day. When I revisit Kingman one day, Smitty's will be my first port of call. But I think I'll leave the cooked skunk for someone else.

With a belly full of food, a new haircut, and a small break in the weather, I decided to do something I hadn't yet had the chance to do in Kansas: go for a walk. The country roads next to our trailer were dead quiet, wide enough, and looked inviting for an afternoon stroll. I recall looking out the window by the trailer and thinking, 'Hmm, it doesn't look too bad, might as well try it'. Off I went, in the direction of the nearby big elevator a couple of miles away. About half a mile from the trailer, the clouds all began to join up and darken. I knew right there and then I had made a bad decision to go off wandering. I turned around and headed back to base. Minutes later, after I thought I might've just gotten away with it, the heavens opened. It rained that hard that I didn't even bother to try and run back. I'd have been soaked anyway. Out of nowhere, a vehicle appeared. I turned and saw Cory and George in the front.

"Need a ride, Paul?" George said, smiling.

"Yes please, thanks George," I said as I climbed in. I told Cory and George I thought it looked like an ok time for a walk so I took my chances, only to get dumped on by the weather in minutes.

George just laughed and said: "Welcome to Kansas!"

Jewell, Kansas

June 2016

It was a standard issue Holland Harvesting move that morning—
up early and on the road. I went about my assigned task of dishes
duty and readied the Lincoln to move out of Kingman. At about
Rice County, I recall seeing a field out the window that I was convinced could've been the spot where the ever-popular Microsoft
'Bliss' image was taken. It stuck out for two reasons. One: because
of its striking resemblance to the image I'd seen so many times, and
two: because the field was not completely flat. For years, 'Bliss' was a
desktop wallpaper image for the Microsoft Windows XP operating
system. It was taken, as I later found out, over west in California
twenty years earlier.

About three-and-a-bit hours later, we arrived in Jewell. I recognised the town square from our comfort stop on the way to Texas
earlier. As it turned out, our camp location in Jewell would be right
by that town square. The connections for water, sewerage, and power
outlets were handily close, and the hard ground meant levelling the
trailer was no trouble. Although I'd carried an adequate supply of

water with me in the car, I was as thirsty as a parched parrot when I was done setting up camp.

I reached into my pocket and slotted a fiver into the vending machine directly over the road. I returned with some Mountain Dew for me and the guys on setup duty. Few drinks in my life have been as refreshing as that one. I met Jeff and Jared, two locals who manned the workshop and gas station where the vending machine was; they were pleasant, welcoming gentlemen. My tractor wasn't at Jewell yet, so with the spare half hour I had, I dashed to the corner store to case it out. It had cheap French vanilla coffee on tap, a new-found favorite of mine, and the owner even looked up my home town on Google Earth. The locals I'd met in Jewell seemed like pretty good sorts.

By the time we'd set up camp and got our trailer in order, it was time to get supper to the field crew who'd already got into the wheat. Sue whipped up a mighty fine lasagne, which we transported to the field in her Ford F-series pickup. Out in the field, just after I'd polished off the lasagne, I met the farmer who we were cutting for. A die-hard Jewell local, he was just as friendly and laid-back as the rest of his fellow community members I'd run into that day. His smile, however, bore an eerie, uncanny resemblance to that of the late actor R. Lee Ermey, perhaps best known for playing Gunnery Sergeant Hartman in the Vietnam war film *Full Metal Jacket*.

I couldn't get the likeness out of my head. The two men were probably similar ages, too. I needed a second opinion. So who better to ask than a U.S. Marine? When Cory got to the field, collected his supper and finished talking to the farmer, I asked him if he was just reminded of the Senior Drill Instructor from *Full Metal Jacket*. He paused, smiled, and said, "Yes, I see it too!"

The farmer had a magnificent-looking house overlooking the field we were cutting which, he told me, was built by a New Zealander. I put it to him that that was the reason why it had come out so good. He smiled and nodded as I gave him my best ambassador's pitch on why he ought to look at coming out to visit New Zealand some time. The house was an archetypal country homestead that, while looking somewhat traditional, had clearly been built in the last decade or so. It featured an old, rustic gas pump outside, a good lawn for a John Deere to cut, and a roomy area out front for vehicles to turn in. As far as Midwest-appropriate houses went, it had to be right up there.

Even though I hadn't done cab time that day, I needed a shower. I found out, on return to the trailer, that we'd be showering in the public facilities in the park within the town square. Apart from looking like a scene location for *Prison Break* it was fairly clean and tidy. The water pressure was good and there was plenty of it. Walking out there with flip-flops, a t-shirt, and a towel felt a little odd for me in June. You'd be a sniffly, sick individual if you tried anything of the sort in New Zealand at that time of year, right in the middle of winter.

A day later, my tractor turned up. It was a relief after a day of running parts and fuel in the heat, which got boring and hot very quickly. Backing it off the trailer wasn't something I'd attempted at that point. Helmer asked if I wanted a go.

"Any last-minute tips?" I asked.

Helmer told me: "Sure, just take it easy and go straight, you'll be fine."

Sure enough, that's all there was to it, except making the forty-foot journey backwards down the incline felt a heck of a lot longer the first time. The field we harvested—shock horror—had some gentle slopes in it. It wasn't very Kansas-like at all. However, like its southern equivalent, the fields of north Kansas were a pleasure to look at and a reminder of why 'Kansas' and 'wheat' will always be common in the same sentence.

I rode shotgun with Rob the next morning. We took the International service truck to the gas station in the nearby town of Randall. I made a donkey of myself when I got the closing mechanism wrong on the diesel nozzle and sent a quick jet of it down the front of my jeans. Roger, the service station owner, called me inside and offered me coffee, donuts, and cream buns.

"Sure," I said and reached for my wallet.

Roger looked at me, bewildered. "No, it's free. Take them for your buddies as well," he told me. I accepted Roger's generous offer and took the sugar-laden treats with me out to the field.

During a field-to-field movement down a farm road, Rob and George exchanged comments over the two-way about a combine operating in a field we passed. I was neither brave enough nor stupid enough to ask what past era that particular model was from. It definitely wasn't built the previous year. Just like the fields from the previous days, those ones actually had some hills. We were well out of T95 radio territory, unfortunately. The only station I could clearly pick up threw out a mix of wholly inoffensive tracks from the late 1990s and early 2000s. While it was a pleasant nostalgic throwback, the songs playing in the cab made me feel like I'd wound up at the supermarket at two on a Saturday afternoon feeling like I had to contemplate where I was going in life. That radio station played the sort of tracks that shopping malls fill their playlists with to create a relaxing atmosphere, encourage shoppers to pretend to feel young again, and avoid calls of complaint from the most easily upset and litigious of customers. I tell 'ya—it was a world away from my usual Staind, Theory of a Deadman, and The Offspring.

On that particular day of harvesting, we were transformed into something of YouTube celebrities. We roaded out to a large, two-sectioned field back near the farmer's house and began to cut away, this time under the watch of a drone. I spotted it hovering around early on and quickly lost sight of it. Little did I know, the remotely-piloted craft was up there for at least an hour recording us in action.

The footage, which is on YouTube for all to see, is truly outstanding and revealing. What it doesn't clearly show is some of the challenges that field presented us. There were some uncomfortably steep slopes at one end of the field. Some of them had an incline that would've at least made me shift my body weight if I rode down them on my dirt bike—a two-stroke, race-bred Honda CR250R motocross speed machine. The middle of the field had a grassed, dipping area which divided the two areas of the field. While it didn't look much from the bird's-eye view in the drone, the operator of the combine or loaded grain cart crossing it had to really watch what they were doing. Anyone who dared cross it too quickly, or at the wrong angle, could've seriously damaged a machine. That day, Helmer's combine was downed by a deer antler, of all things. A fellow operator asked Helmer if the angle of his machine "felt funny". It sure as hell didn't look right. Kelvin asked on the radio if Helmer "had that sinking feeling" before the #4 combine man got out and discovered a deer antler had gone straight through one of his float tyres.

A day or few passed by. While I saw quite a few deer strolling around checking us out, no more of their discarded antlers held us up. We tackled fields with terraces, turns, abandoned houses—some probably from the Dust Bowl era—and ups and downs. Parked all by its lonesome, next to our field, sat some farmhand's pickup. Convinced I hadn't seen one like it before, I asked on the radio for "one of you American boys" to please identify what it was. It took Clint all of about two seconds to confirm it was a slightly modified Chevy Silverado, maybe twelve or so years old. I liked the look of it.

The wheat seemed to hold up pretty well. The truck drivers had life a little easier on that job, as the farmer had his own elevator setup and a trusty young man running it. A nephew or grandson of his, we believed. We didn't care. The kid was efficient, switched on, and he did the job just fine. With such varied, non-typical landscapes to harvest, the days went by in a flash and seemed to be over quicker than they began. I felt the time appear to speed up. That meant a pretty tired me at the end of the day. I never had trouble falling asleep at night during Harvest 2016. Especially not in Jewell.

I think on our last day harvesting in Jewell we just might've sailed pretty close to the wind. I'm not going to say the grain was wet, but, at a guess, it would've only been just inside the moisture range that was typically allowed at a public elevator. But hey, it was the farmer's grain, the farmer's elevator, and, therefore, the farmer's rules! We burned diesel far earlier than usual that morning as we raced against the impending weather front. It looked like it was going to bucket down any moment. We saw the end in sight and went for it while we could. The field had some odd-shaped gullies, turns, terraces, and multiple entry points. That kept it interesting for the truckers and grain cart operators. The field was so varied, it would've been fun to tear apart on a dirt bike. After we finished the mix-and-match field we headed back to the farmer's yard to blow off and load the combines for the road ahead.

The forecast and visible rain on the horizon eventually came around. Fortunately for us, we'd already cleaned and loaded the machines. With the rain, after it cleared, came an hour or two off. I changed out of my work gear and went for a stroll around Jewell. There were dogs barking everywhere. None of them seemed malnourished or ill-treated. I thought they were probably just bored as hell. There were hardly any passing cars for them to bark at, let alone a foreigner wandering the sidewalk.

Later that afternoon we were treated to a personally guided tour of Roy Arasmith's Antique Toy Collection. It was like no other toy collection I'd ever seen. I spotted a few of the same 1950s- and 60s-era Tonka toys my dad and uncle passed down to me, as well as later-model die-cast examples and pedal-car-sized moving models. I am confident in saying it would be one of the more comprehensive agricultural and industrial-related toy and model collections on the planet. If you go by Jewell one day, call in. Ask if you can have a look around. But, be warned—your travel partners or your insurance agent will probably end up having to drag you out of the place. It's outstanding!

We were ready to move west. But one of the Kenworth truck's motors was heating up like the business end of a Cuban cigar. It was parked up at a storage yard along the highway at McDonald, KS. Earlier in the day, that truck and several others were driven to that yard, which was something of a rally point on the way to Colorado, our next destination. Rob ferried a carload of us out there and, in the scorching heat, we got to work and removed the radiator so it could be blown out and cleaned up. It took a couple of hours to knock the job on the head. A couple of guys, myself included, stole a nap on the way home. I was awake, however, when we travelled through the town of Smith Center, a short distance from the geographical center of the contiguous United States.

Eads, Colorado

June 2016

To confirm what we'd heard talk of a day or two earlier, we were off to Cory's home state of Colorado. I didn't know there even was harvesting in Colorado. About all I knew about the state, thanks to popular culture and my own lack of knowledge of anything Colorado-related, was that it was all mountains, marijuana, the Broncos, and *South Park*. To my delight, Cory informed me there was indeed a place in Colorado named South Park. To my dismay, I learned it wasn't that close to the place where we'd be going to harvest, Eads. A new state was a bonus to me. I hadn't known before I'd arrived in the United States that I'd get the chance to visit Colorado. I counted myself lucky.

As soon as we crossed the state line into Colorado, the drug jokes and stereotypes flew around on the two-way. I looked out the window of the Lincoln I was driving. I wondered how, even if you tried, you could manage to grow anything in the place. It was desolate. There was just—well, absolutely nothing. I knew the good farmland was somewhere out there. It was kind of obvious on the way in that we hadn't got to it yet, unless we planned on harvesting tumbleweeds and hard rock to turn a profit. But still, we were in a new state.

The crew locked into another race against the weather. An ugly-looking storm was brewing. We were right in town, in something of a mini trailer park. All the facilities' hook-ups were close by. We set up camp as quickly as we could, minus a few guys who were still on the road shifting machinery, and minus Tommy, who'd been drafted to help on another farm. Another truck still had radiator issues. When we pulled the unit off, we saw just why. It was plugged to hell. After a running repair on the Kenworth's dusty radiator, Rob dashed to the township and fetched us a burger feed. We chowed down on that before the rain encircled us overhead and forced a retreat indoors.

In Colorado, our machinery yard was about twenty miles from camp. The highway out there snaked through a desolate, shrub-covered landscape that looked as hospitable as a planet from outer space. The drive was something of a novelty the first time, but we all knew it was going to turn into a drive we would grow tired of soon, especially at the end of a fifteen-hour haul. As we got closer to Haswell, CO, where the machinery sat, the land began to look like crop country. There were some combines dotted here and there on the horizon, reportedly belonging to our fellow northern Midwestern contemporaries, Brown Harvesting, who were based out of Devils Lake, North Dakota.

Out at the yard, we fuelled up and got into it. It was at least a forty-minute trip out to the fields to have a look. The landscape was super flat and like nothing I'd ever seen before. There wasn't a large tree in sight. There were no gullies, no undulations, no real landmarks. Other than the crop, there wasn't really anything out there at all. The wheat looked half decent. I un-tarped my cart and headed out into the field with Rob to give it a whirl. The sample didn't make the grade. Neither did the one we took a few hours later. Becoming almost traditional by that point, the sky held what looked like the beginnings of another storm. On return to the trailer for the second time that day, it still hadn't rained. I ventured out and braved a small walk around the block. If there was a 'No Engine Brakes' bylaw in Eads, few truck drivers gave a stuff about it. I heard more Jake brakes clattering away on that walk than I did standing out at our field next to the Interstate 44 in Texas. Anticipating rain, we fastened up our trailer fittings before settling into a crew screening of *American Sniper.*

Although it didn't rain overnight, we found out we weren't cutting the next morning. A few of us took the opportunity to zip down to the general store and stock up on lunch provisions. We got what we needed, including a can of some dodgy-looking 'sleep drink' which promised the consumer relaxing, drawn-out dreams. 'Why not?' I thought. It could be the best seventy-five cents I'd spend. The rest of the day was spent diving, flipping, and goofing around in the local pool, located only a few hundred feet from the trailer. That pool complex didn't really have rules. As long as we didn't land *on* anyone, the lifeguard said, we could pretty much do whatever we wanted. I managed a back-flip off the diving board, something that had taken me more than twenty-eight years to complete! The next day was more or less a repeat of the day before it, except that night we drove down to Lamar, a nearby Walmart-sized town. I picked up Metallica and Kid Rock CDs for the tractor. Perfect ammunition to deploy against fatigue.

Although we got caned by the rain overnight, we soldiered out to the field and gave it a crack in the afternoon. At first, it went just fine. The fields were long, rectangular and fairly smooth. You had to watch carefully which row you chose to hop on, as it was close to a mile to the other end. It was an excellent field in which to be a grain cart operator. Unfortunately, nature didn't see it that way. A few hours in, the meanest-looking storm since Kansas enveloped the sky and forced us to idle down and tarp up, bringing with it a tiresome dose of rain. We were going to be off the diesel for at least forty-eight hours. In the meantime, we were granted leave to head over and check out Colorado Springs.

A two-and-a-bit hour drive from Eads, Colorado Springs is a picturesque, tree-lined city nestled at the foot of the Rocky Mountains. Perched over than a mile above sea level, it's home to more than 400,000 residents and several significant military installations. I took it all in like a sponge. To legitimize our commonly-held marijuana jokes and stereotypes, we saw a number of weed outlets with some genuinely laughable puns and slogans to boost sales.

First on the agenda was the Cheyenne Mountain Zoo. Up behind the city, on the slopes of Cheyenne Mountain itself, the zoo sure was something different from the days out in the fields. We saw tigers, hippos, giraffes, elephants, and wallabies. Zoos are always going to be the subject of many a debate on ethics, and the rights and wrongs of captivity. What I did observe at Cheyenne Mountain Zoo was what appeared to be a culture of placing animal wellbeing high up the list of priorities, as well as education. At every enclosure, there was a sizable board of information for attendees to take in. I soaked up as much of the board content as I could, only to be terrified by the Burmese python that was slithering about in its enclosure. Nearby, a zoo staff member was holding a snake out in the open. It was about three feet long and it had a small crowd of on-lookers staring right at it. If you wanted, you could go and hold the snake, which appeared to be unfazed by it all. Presumably, it wasn't in a swallowing or strangling kind of mood. The zoo staffer asked if I'd like to hold the serpent. I'd have rather held a grenade after the pin was pulled.

After a trip down the hill from the zoo and an outstanding burger meal at Sonic, we headed out of town to a shooting range. I chose three weapons: an M16 rifle, an MP5 submachine gun (both capable of firing on full automatic mode), and a P30 pistol. Although I wanted to try out a .45 caliber model, we had a discount on buying ammo. To me, it made sense to get something that shot the same 9mm rounds as the MP5.

I presented my New Zealand Firearms Licence to the range personnel, signed the necessary forms, and headed on through. The firing range was exactly what you might expect: a sterile-looking, well-lit room with metal sidings to separate you from the next booth, and polished concrete floors covered in empty shell casings. It reminded me of the hazard course area you encounter in the opening stages of the video game *Half-Life*. I chatted to the range instructor while I loaded the M16 magazine with 5.56 mm rounds before I ordered my target down-range. The M16 was heavier than I'd imagined. It wasn't hard to move around, but I'd just held on to this idea over the years that it was a bit lighter. After a few rounds on semi-automatic, I double-checked with the instructor if I could shift the selector lever to full-automatic, or 'full retard', as he called it. He nodded. I flicked it to face back to 'AUTO' and opened fire.

I had enough 9mm for one full magazine in the MP5 sub-machine gun, and about a magazine-and-a-half in the pistol. Holding, shouldering, and firing the MP5 was everything I'd come to expect, speaking as someone from the generation introduced to the video game *Counter-Strike* and 1990s James Bond films at an impressionable age. The weapon was light, easy to move around, and boy was it quick to get through the ammo. Just like the M16, the MP5 was quite something to shoot on full auto.

On to the P30. I slid the pistol magazine in and chambered a round. My target was at ten meters for the first five or six rounds, then back at about twenty meters for the remainder. My shot grouping wasn't as tight as I felt it should've been, but the main objective was achieved: I had fun. A Heckler & Koch P30 isn't something you just find lying around, so I was happy enough I got the chance to fire one and experience it all. I watched Clint get off the last of his pistol rounds in a lane two over from me. He did not look like a man firing a handgun for the first time. Right across the carpark from the shooting range was a Bass Pro Shops store. I'd heard all about the place from some of the guys on the crew. We had an hour or so to kill, so we all headed on over and wandered around. Even the store-brand hats looked really good. I bought a *his & hers* matching pair for Mum and Dad back home.

Back across state in Eads, it was raining. *Again.* The plus side? We found out we had the opportunity to return to Colorado Springs for another day to look around and to stay the night. We had a choice for the next forty-eight hours: sit in a rained-out trailer park in a far-flung town, or have another look around a military city with someone who used to live near it. Cory, the Colorado native, said he'd like to go with, and that he could show us around a few haunts and sights in the place. It took me all of about one second to make up my mind. The 'shotgun' rule, governing who got the front seat in the car, was still at play. That time, I managed to get lucky and score a front seat in the Lincoln with Cory at the wheel.

On the drive back to Colorado Springs, Cory pointed out a number of places he remembered from his formative years in the state. We drove near the road to his childhood home and past sports fields of yesteryear. We talked shop about his service in the Marine Corps. I enjoyed listening to Cory's accounts of his assignments at home and abroad. As we drew closer to Colorado Springs, we discussed the missions of the various military sites there. Amongst other things, we speculated about what may or may not be going on inside the Cheyenne Mountain Complex, a secretive installation buried deep within the slopes of the mountain. On behalf of the group, Cory made a phone call to the United States Air Force Academy, a picturesque installation outside Colorado Springs where the Air Force trains its officers. To my delight, we would be permitted to head inside for a tour of the facility later on.

The United States Air Force Academy appeared to have not only a training mission but a public relations mission as well. I thought, on arrival at the academy, both those missions appeared to be ticking along just fine. The immaculately-kept, sprawling grounds went right to the edge of the Rocky Mountains. The place had numerous sports fields for multiple codes, incredible views of the surrounding environment, and its very own football stadium, which was visible from the nearby highway. As far as living and training in a military environment went, the academy didn't look half bad. We were given free rein to wander around parts of the academy and take it all in. Despite the overcast and slightly chilly weather, it was a brilliant day out.

On return to Eads, a few of us went along to a local church service. We heard from Nathan and Yuka Williams about their mission to spread the Christian gospel in Japan. I had the chance to speak with Nathan after the service about what sounded like an infinitely complex and challenging task. Soon after, we got word from Devin that the local newspaper wanted to interview our crew. We chatted to the reporter about the harvest, our backgrounds, and the journey so far. Cassie, the consistent comedian, jokingly—and very loudly— proclaimed he was "an illegal" in the United States. That made it into the newspaper report. Ironically, the reporter appeared to have misheard him and wrote in the story that Cassie was a 'legal' resident in the United States. While that was in fact the case, it certainly made for a laugh. On a rainy morning a day or so later, we called into a nearby gas station for coffee and cigars. The woman at the counter recognised us and said we could not leave the premises until we all signed her copy of the paper. We the 'Wheaties', as we were called, had apparently made quite the name for ourselves.

As the rain cleared and we fell back into harvest, the Fourth of July rolled around. The fields were long, rectangular, and dusty. They were smooth and allowed for relatively easy, stress-free loading of trucks. Eads and Haswell both put on fireworks displays for the big night. Apart from our machines, there was no other light pollution. We saw both towns' efforts, live from the field.

During harvest, a tense moment or day could change tack at a moment's notice. A comment or a funny observation could evaporate a stressed situation on the spot. Although this example was definitely one for the 'you really had to be there' files, it's too good not to recall. We'd had a fairly good day's harvest, but we had to pull up earlier than expected. We'd finished, parked up and idled down. We were ready to head back to base. We stood in a half circle around Rob, who'd just briefed us on field movements, truck locations, and how the next couple of runs would go. He'd given a detailed description of the routes we'd need to take.

Rob was clear on what he wanted to happen, but I don't think I was the only one who mentally repeated the battle plan to memorize it, only because the roads to the surrounding fields typically weren't labelled, and were so flat they made Iowa look like the Himalayas. Plus, we were in a remote area that was at least twenty miles from the nearest town with more than one store. Silence took over for a good few seconds.

Then Tennessee Jake said, "So we're gonna take the route to get from our elbow to our thumb?"

We all froze, looked at Jake and wrinkled our faces. Rob shot Jake a look and half-said, half-questioned: "*What?!*"

We all burst out laughing. We were hysterical. I think we even got a chuckle out of Rob with that one.

Onida, South Dakota

July 2016

The night before we left for South Dakota, I found out I'd be driving the boss's own Dodge Ram 2500 pickup. That came with a degree of responsibility. I would, at times, scout up front to act as a lookout and pilot driver. Not only was Rob's pickup truck a hell of a nice vehicle to drive, it also came with a working subscription to Sirius satellite radio. I kept it tuned to *80s on 8* for most of the journey. I was treated to a bit of Van Halen, Phil Collins, and tracks from an assortment of artists from my decade of birth. I hauled the fuel bowser behind the pickup, so I made use of the vehicle's standard-feature exhaust brake system. It was impressive—so quiet you could barely hear it.

When we hit Nebraska I noticed, once again, that it was not the broad, flat landscape that stereotypes had promised me. That corner of the state was hilly and rough. Much of it was, like I noted weeks earlier, similar to bits of New Zealand. We passed Lake McConaughy. Party and holiday mode was in full swing. There were people show-boating and frolicking in the water, families picnicking, and Jet Skis roaring about on the lake. Lake McConaughy seemed like a popular

Midwest destination for a summer getaway. I was enjoying driving the pickup and I was eager to see South Dakota. But I had to say, a blast around the water on a Jet Ski would've been fun.

We were well into the heart of Nebraska when I had to pull over to refuel. The pickup trucks each had a tank, full of clear diesel, that sat on the tray at the back. I radioed the convoy to advise them of my movements and pulled up in an open lot behind a gas station. I went about refuelling as quickly as I could. I didn't want to be separated from the convoy for long. The radio signal was patchy, and the mobile phone reception was dodgy at best. As I refuelled, I watched what I believed was a local family as they walked into the gas station. There were two young children; they looked like they were right out of a Cavender's catalogue. Their mom followed behind. She had platinum blonde hair, wore a flannel shirt, cowboy boots, and looked about twenty-three. She would have stood 5'1" on a good day and weighed 130 pounds soaking wet. Then the husband wandered in—he would've weighed over 250 lbs and stood at least 6'5". He had shoulders wider than the front of a pickup truck I was driving. I moved my head ever so slightly so it appeared as though I was refuelling, not people-watching. Nebraska, huh.

When we got to Onida, South Dakota, I was impressed. The farmland was magnificent. I bet some good land there wasn't cheap. The water on tap was fresh and ice-cold, and we had several bars of 4G reception. My phone's signal had spat the dummy in Colorado, so connectivity again was a real plus. When we first got to Texas I felt a good vibe in the air. When we arrived in Onida, I felt a different vibe. It sure was a positive one. I liked it there already. I could feel it. Onida sits roughly in the middle of South Dakota, about forty minutes north of the state capital, Pierre. I discussed the 'Onida vibe' with a crew member some time after harvest. He, too, said he knew he was keen on the place right from the word go.

Another bonus was the location of our camp. Compared to the daily trek from the machinery yard to camp in Colorado, which was close to forty miles there and back, our trek for much of our swing in Onida was about 200 feet. We had a pre-set area to assemble our trailers, park up, and unload the machines for easy and close access. After our routine setup we got busy with some light servicing, general maintenance, and check-ups. I consulted my tractor manual and gave the torque wrench a good workout.

That night we were released to Pierre for supper. Pierre is a very pleasant city with all the usual haunts for a harvest crew on the move: big hardware stores, a great Walmart, and quality steak houses. That night's choice was Mad Mary's. Being in South Dakota, I decided to support a local rancher and order an 18oz steak, complete with an onion soup starter. It was great. Mad Mary's went down well with everyone. We called into Walmart on the way home for provisions. Mine included Van Halen's 'best-of' CD and a pack of Bud Light Platinum. *Just like a local*, my recently-wed friend at home, Waata, remarked on Facebook when I posted an image of those items.

Up and into it the next day, we fired up the machines and had a crack at the field which surrounded our campsite. The moisture was a little high. It forced us to retire to an early lunch. The July sun sorted that out quick enough. By that afternoon we had a couple of machines away and cutting. I have to say again, the South Dakota countryside was incredible. Although we were in a big, flat field that could be mistaken, at a glance, for any of the multitudes of other fields we would cut, there was just something different about South Dakota. In my tractor, with my new Van Halen CD pumping out 'Dreams', 'Jump!' and other assorted favorites of mine, I couldn't help but look and marvel at the land in every direction. It was a treat—an honor.

It was right as I was about to tuck into my supper when I saw it. Just over my shoulder to the south. There was an enormous plume of smoke, spewing out of a nearby field. It was no boy-scout campfire. I had just collected a load of grain from a combine heading out north, so I swung around for a closer look. In that ten-odd seconds, the smoke had thickened and risen. I radioed Rob immediately and told him what I was seeing. I believe a resident farm worker, who was riding along with us that evening, had just seen it as well and had, moments earlier, ordered a water truck headed right that way. I found it difficult to tell exactly how far away the blaze was. I would have guessed it was about a mile or two. It was terrifying how quickly the inferno grew.

Every harvester has heard stories about and seen photos of what can happen when something catches fire. Seeing it happen relatively close by was a real eye-opener. As far as I know, we never found out exactly what started that fire. It could have been any number of things, such as a mechanical fault on a field machine, a pickup driving in the stubble, or a tossed cigarette, to name a few. The fire was quickly extinguished. Thankfully, it didn't burn out of control.

The cutting went fairly well throughout the next few days. The moisture did tend to hang around a wee bit in the morning and slow things by maybe half an hour or so. The local rock radio station, Capital City Rock, was a real find. It played AC/DC, Puddle of Mudd, Shinedown, and a good selection of hard rock, mainly from the 1990s, 2000s, and the current decade. The station offered some rather interesting thoughts in between songs and advertisements. One example was that if you, the listener, were to rob a bank, you'd be sorted. You would never have to worry about bills ever again. You would either become wealthy all of a sudden, or you would spend the rest of your time behind bars. Life advice can be found in the most unexpected of places.

The next morning, it was immediately clear it was too moist to cut right away. Tony and I got straight to work with the air compressor to blow out our filters and cabs. If you put your mind to it for ten minutes, you could transform your cab into an entirely different place. Tony and I both tried to keep our cabs as clean as possible. However, as grain cart operators, we'd have to enter and exit the cab frequently, often to help dole out meals on the go in the field, which was a daily duty of ours. With the never-ending wheat dust, there was only so much you could do to keep the cab completely clean. I must've cleaned my cab dozens of times throughout the season. I still remember that morning, clear as day. I was leaning over into the cab going at it while 'Asking for It' by Shinedown was playing away in the background. I also ate all my snacks way too early.

We burned a lot of diesel that week. Other than the slower mornings, the weather was gracious to us. The machines performed well and the wheat was outstanding. South Dakota is prime harvesting country and boy did it show. We worked hard; it was hot, we were tired—but we were all enjoying going hammer and tongs to get the crop off. Once we finished all the nearby fields that were ready to cut, we got instructions to prepare the machines to road north. Destination: Gettysburg, SD. My loud "four score and seven grains ago" response to this news, with most of the crew present, fell on unappreciative ears. As it happened, Gettysburg had a sign on the way in which reads: *Gettysburg—where the battle wasn't.* I made a point to get a photo of it. A snapshot for the harvest album!

Roading machinery was something I always enjoyed. You got to see a new bit of the countryside while you sailed along at a comfortable pace. There was no stress, nothing to worry about. All you had to do was watch what you were doing, listen to the two-way, and enjoy the ride. The people in the Midwest localities we worked in, Onida and Gettysburg included, were clearly used to seeing tractors and combines on the road. No-one was in a hurry. Everyone pulled over, waited patiently, and waved as we passed by. There were no stupid passing maneuvers, no horn blasts, and generally no signs of people in cars wanting to do anything dumb. The locals knew: it was harvest season; there were machines, and if they waited about thirty seconds they could pass or speed up at free will.

The land out beyond Gettysburg had undulating plains. It was equally impressive as its Sully County equivalent back toward Onida. The crops looked great. The scores of nearby lakes were picturesque. In general, it all looked mighty fine—like it belonged on a table placemat or a showcase corporate photograph in an agriculture store. As we went about firing up the machines and getting the relocated harvest underway, 104.5FM continued to play more Puddle of Mudd. That band, a long-time favorite of mine, performs many good songs other than the famous 'Blurry' track. I was thrilled to see a radio station recognise that with its actions. On the way back to camp we were told breakfast would be at 8:30. Although I hadn't touched a drop of liquor in days, I barely remember getting in bed or sleeping that night. I guess I must've really needed it.

The next day at Gettysburg, while performing a routine truck-load, I felt my left side sink. I continued the unload to remove as much weight as possible from my tractor and trailer combination before getting out. The inevitable had happened: I'd run over a shed deer antler and done a tire. I limped my machine back to the staging area. A few minutes earlier, I'd met up with Michael, a friend from New Zealand who was in the area. I'd let him know where we were in case he could show up, and show up he did. I remember Michael's New Zealand accent sounded put on. Almost fake. Apart from talking on the phone to Mum and Dad, I hadn't heard another Kiwi for months. It was good—a small reminder of home from the other side of the world. It was a pity he'd joined me in my tractor only minutes before it was kneecapped by a deer antler.

In the morning I headed off with Helmer to go and fetch my tractor. I had planned it all out the night before. I would take a photo of the antler next to the tractor, under tire repair, and post something to Facebook. It didn't quite go to plan. When we arrived the tire guy was almost done. He was a burly Wisconsin native who was twice my size.

"Hey man, whereabouts did that deer antler get to?" I asked.

He responded, quietly and curtly, "What deer antler?"

I got the message. Whatever happened to the deer antler, I wasn't getting it. And my much-planned and thought-about Facebook post and Snapchat was not going to happen. I thanked the tire guy, idled up, and set off on the journey to join the crew at the next field.

It was an odd feeling roading alone. I had my beacon and flashers on, but not having the crew rolling with me, it wasn't the same. That wasn't the only reason the trip was memorable. When I got to the big T-junction close to our new field, a red vehicle pulled out from behind me and sped off, leaning on its horn, just as I was about to make the turn. I put two and two together. The car must've been right behind me for quite some time. The driver was pissed. The car blended in with the big red cart behind me. I knew I'd checked my mirrors, as always, and I wasn't crawling along too slow either.

When I was done irritating local motorists, I arrived at the new field. It was mega. You could've fit all of New Zealand and some of Australia inside it and still have room to spare. Its slight undulation meant you couldn't quite see one end from the other. The two-way radio was my friend in that field. Rather, it was pretty much my compass. The two-way was the only way to 100 percent know where everyone was. That field was just the type I had imagined when I pictured Harvest America in my head before I flew out; it wasn't something I would ever forget.

By breakfast time the following morning, the temperature had already reached what our crew would classify as 'hot as *balls*' (best heard in Tennessee Jake's accent and humorous tone). The humidity in the air temporarily halted us. Even as we blew out filters and readied cabs, the guys' phone app temperatures were reading 104F. That's forty degrees Celsius—hot in almost anyone's book. That day's searing heat might have contributed to Devin blowing out one of his hopper bottom trailer tires. When we heard on the two-way what he'd done, Jake chimed in: "Can't afford another one of them sum'bitches." Those of us who heard that comment in Kansas burst out laughing. The rest of the crew must've wondered what had possessed Jake.

All of us who'd tuned into Capital City Rock that day heard the story of an elderly woman in England. She fought off a would-be attacker in a supermarket with a leg of ham. The radio's account of the situation was that the woman turned upon the would-be assailant and went at him for all money with the delicatessen item until he backed off. I forget who, but one of the crew said on the radio, "Did you guys hear that?" We chimed in, laughing, that yes, we had heard it. Rob asked what we were on about. Tony recounted the story and labelled the woman of the hour as 'the pork pummeler'.

Our downhill run at the business end of our swing in Onida was about to slow down. Late one afternoon we found out that Tony's tractor had sheared a couple of bolts. That meant we were down to one cart for half a dozen combines. It didn't halt the operation entirely, but it certainly did put the brakes on it. Tony was faster and more skilled than me as a grain cart operator. I did my best to keep up, which I did most of the time, but we missed Tony like an engine misses its oil—hours seem like minutes when you're the only cart operator. That said, it always helped to have great music on in the background. Capital City Rock took care of that. Later in the evening, Sue put together a pork supper, complete with a cheese and potato dish, and some home-made dessert.

When we'd cut the last of our wheat for the time being, Rob and Sue had to briefly shoot back to Minnesota. We geared up and headed out past Gettysburg to blow off combines and prepare for a move. I teamed up with Kelvin in my dust-killing kit. It consisted of a U.S. military-issue top, leather gloves, my desert camo hat, and a harvest dust mask. We readied the machines and knocked out the job over a couple of hours. I got the chance to move a couple of the combines around, which was fun. We did this all in a finished field, right next to a fall crop plantation and a lake. It was a nice setting for some hot, dirty work. After that, we roaded the machines to the staging area at Gettysburg to be loaded onto trucks. Some hilarious radio banter played out on the way; I feel for anyone who might've listened in on our channel that afternoon.

The next morning's truck loading was over quickly and went exactly to plan. A handful of us were a bit dusty. We'd enjoyed a few drinks by the trailer the night before in a much-needed session to blow off some steam. The lingering beers aside, we had the machines strapped, chained, and ready to head north to the Bakken in no time. Our departure from South Dakota was imminent. But before we left The Mount Rushmore State there was one ritual yet to be undertaken: Cattleman's Club Steakhouse.

No trip to central South Dakota is complete without a meal at Cattleman's. There was sawdust on the floor, a bar stocked with numerous alcoholic necessities, and a great selection of South Dakota cuisine, all to be enjoyed with a view across the Missouri River. Some might say you aren't supposed to order a T-bone steak at a specialist joint. Stuff that. I was so hungry I was considering going to work on one of my limbs. The T-bone option seemed like and tasted like a good idea. Later in the season we would return to Cattleman's. I know I certainly will when I return to South Dakota.

One the way home we called into Runnings. Visiting big hardware stores in the United States is an experience in its own right. Wherever we journeyed, we routinely called into hardware stores for a look around. These mega-markets stocked firearms, a wide range of clothing, tools, candy, and all kinds of weird and wonderful goods. I took turns with Kelvin holding a Desert Eagle pistol. Those things are *big*. I left the store with a new John Deere hoodie and a camouflage John Deere cap I'd never seen before. Another for my collection!

Regent, North Dakota

August 2016

Once again, it was moving day. The drill was familiar by then. We loaded as many machines and implements as we could carry, got jacked up on coffee, and talked about various stereotypes and expectations of the place we are about to visit. My contribution to the North Dakota discussion was that as well as wheat, there was a lot of oil and nuclear weapons in the ground.

I drove north in the Lincoln Town Car with Helmer. We discussed buying and selling cars and bikes, and the weird and wonderful characters you meet when doing so. Helmer was rightly shocked about how much cars cost in New Zealand compared to the United States. Back in Kansas, we'd seen advertisements for perfectly reasonable Chevrolet Corvettes and Ford Mustangs that were only a few years old for well under $10,000 (in both New Zealand and United States dollar amounts). That would be as rare as rocking horse dung in New Zealand. Cars have quite a long trip all the way down to New Zealand and there will only ever be so many available. The price is always going to be higher—definitely more than in the Midwest.

The further north we went, the more remote the landscape looked. The geographic changes were slow and subtle, but noticeable. I felt like we were entering something of the 'wild west' of the Midwest region. There were more fenced-off fields with stock grazing. We didn't see as much of that further south. The land was rougher and tougher. There were lots of sunflowers. We saw a small house with a few sheep nearby. I told Kelvin it was wonderful the New Zealand Government had gone to such great lengths to locate its embassy and consulate all the way up there in North Dakota. That's what I call diplomacy for the ages!

About four hours after leaving Onida we made it to our new town, Regent. It's a small farming center with a purpose-built feel to it. In and around the town there were all sorts of crops, nearly ready to be harvested. We saw canola, sunflowers, and varieties of wheat. Our base in Regent was a caravan park just behind the main street. It was near a gas station, a vending machine, and the pub. Readily available alcohol and a machine to service my penchant for Diet Mountain Dew was just great. Sue prepared us a feed of nachos for supper before some of us ventured into the pub for a few quiets.

I paid about six dollars for two beers. Value aside, I got talking to the bartender about rock music. Originally from Seattle, Washington, the bartender really knew his stuff. He talked about seeing Nirvana, Soundgarden, and Alice in Chains, well before any of those bands made it big. He mentioned where Kurt Cobain's house was, seeing Chris Cornell play in, quite literally, a garage show, and numerous other gigs and goings-on from that landmark grunge rock period in the early 1990s. I was a little sceptical at first. To a fellow grunge rock enthusiast, it all seemed a little too good to be true. However, with the detail the guy went into, his apparent age, and how relaxed and passionate he was about it all, I believed it probably added up. Then he gave me the frequency for the local rock music station. It played lots of AC/DC, Breaking Benjamin, Green Day, and Soundgarden. Perfect.

Early the next morning I thought I had started the custom harvesting equivalent of a Mexican standoff. We'd unloaded and parked our equipment at this place that was sort of like a village green for harvest machinery. Other custom cutters had done the same thing. Everyone had their gear lined up for servicing, ready to roll out to the field. My tractor and cart combination was, in length and by dimension, the biggest piece of field machinery we had. I'd just taken it off the trailer and looked for a park. The only spot I could see was a few meters from the rest of our gear, right over next to another crew's. All of their equipment was shiny, green and yellow John Deere machinery. I crept over and parked as unobtrusively as I could manage. That was right when the head honcho of the crew turned around and made a beeline straight for me.

I thought he was about to tell me to move my machine someplace else. By all rights, I sort of was in his crew's area. It was also clear I didn't really have anywhere else to go. The conversation was something I won't forget. It went like this:

"Hey. You're from the Holland crew, right?"

"Yes, sir!"

"You must've washed those windows and that paintwork down real good, right?"

"Uh, yeah?" I agreed, wondering what on Earth he was getting at.

"Well y'all washed them so good the whole thing has turned green and into a John Deere!"

We both burst out laughing as I caught on to his joke. Because I'd fallen in with his crew's parking area, he'd claimed that tractor of ours as one of his, even swapping its manufacturer in the process. I should never have doubted him. Of course, he saw I parked in the only safe and practicable spot. I showed him my John Deere-branded holster with my wrench and knife to let him know I appreciated the pro green-and-yellow sentiment.

We fuelled up and roaded the machinery out into the countryside. The move to the new section took us about forty minutes. That bit of North Dakota had gentle, rolling plains. While I wouldn't have called it hilly, at least not by New Zealand standards, it wasn't nearly as flat as Kansas or Colorado, and it had something of a rough and ready feel about it. Most fields we drove past had at least some grade of slope in them. We weren't far from South Dakota. The land in North Dakota looked completely different. It wasn't really much like anything I had seen on the trip so far.

Tony's cart was still in the hurt locker. That day it was Paul David Savage from Whanganui, New Zealand, versus five combines. The local radio pumped out industrial levels of Nirvana, Green Day, and Red Hot Chili Peppers as I blasted around the field trying to keep everyone empty. I wasn't Tony, but I hadn't been on the cart for five minutes, either. I'd finally managed to build a bank of confidence and experience. Bar one or two minor stoppages, I kept everyone moving that day. I loaded and dispatched almost forty trucks in that late morning and afternoon. A benefit of that situation was that four hours seems like about forty minutes. And it's always a plus when you have some great rock music to go with. Best of all? We heard that night that Tony's machine was about to come back into service. Not a minute too soon!

The previously balmy North Dakota weather gave way. By our next afternoon on the job, the sky had darkened. Rob instructed us to get into formation and park up. Cart operators would also ensure they tarped up their carts to keep the payload dry. Once or twice during harvest, I had a horrible feeling I hadn't tarped the cart. I would turn around and go back, or ask another crew member if they could. It didn't happen to me that day, fortunately. One time later it did, though. On the way back into town, Rob took us up a small mountain of sorts. At the top of it was a cellular phone tower and some other communications equipment. It had an excellent view over the whole town and a good section of the surrounding properties. The small mountain, if you took away the comms equipment, was not unlike a landmark in New Zealand called Mount Wellington which, as it happens, is in Auckland, not the capital city of Wellington, with which it shares a name.

The unexpectedly early finish that day somehow drained me of my energy. I felt shattered. Normally at about two or three in the afternoon I was as energetic as ever and right on the ball. Not that day. I strolled up to grab a French vanilla. The stores were closed, but the Enchanted Highway Gift Shop was open. It boasted some large, perversely impressive scrap-metal sculptures. Aside from its weird and wonderful selection of locally-forged creations, it had tasty ice cream. I wolfed one down and went for a second, because *why not?* I sat out the front and ate the thing like I wanted diabetes by dark. I saw a few of the crew drive past. The red Dodge pickup swung around, parked up front, and out climbed half a dozen of the boys. Clint told me later the conversation inside the pickup had gone something like this: "Hey that looks like Paul ... Wait, it is Paul. Paul has ice cream. Let's get ice cream too!"

The following morning we broke rhythm. Cory, Rob, and Tony headed down to go and fetch the now-repaired grain cart from South Dakota. The rest of us got a gig hauling wheat. I moved between trucks to assist where I could before I found myself a job running the crank. That involved standing next to the slide-out auger—the spiralling, spinning piece of metal which zips the grain up from ground level and into the storage facility—and guiding the truck driver as they reversed into position. When the truck's hopper bottom opening was in line with the auger, I would signal to the driver to halt before I opened up the hatch, using the crank, and made sure the grain fell in the right place at the right rate. I would repeat this process for the next compartment. Each trailer had two compartments. It was menial, low brain activity compared to the hustle of racing around in the cart. Time slowed down. But I learned something new and enjoyed myself.

The change in scene continued. As soon as the muggy morning allowed, we drove further into the countryside and switched to durum wheat. The durum grain, used for the production of pasta, is larger and heavier than the typical wheat grain you might picture. We hit the field, loaded up, and took samples. While we waited for the sample info to come back so we could fire up again, I noticed several groups of beehives. My cousin, Phil, had gotten right into his beekeeping over the last couple of years. I'd even gone along with him once to check out how it all worked. I've been good buddies with Phil since the day we met. Over the years we have always been in touch via MSN, Facebook, and whatever technology of the day we decided to use. I sent Phil a Snapchat of what I'd seen. He correctly guessed there were a lot of sunflowers nearby. When the durum wheat sample returned we shut down—a few of those pasta dishes would have to wait.

That afternoon we were back to trucking. I rode along with Helmer to an elevator setup about forty-five minutes away. As I recall, it was south-west of Regent. I don't remember it being on the edge of, or in, a town or city, so I can't give an exact location. Although if I was in Regent today, I'm sure I could drive to it. That elevator was awesome. At most of them, the driver would need to exit the cab to crank open the hopper bottom. Not so at that place. You entered the complex via a long, wide roadway complete with drive-on scales and a receipt printer. Minus the silos, it looked like a recently-built milking shed you might see in New Zealand's Waikato or Taranaki regions. When you got to the pull-up area, an attendant would un-crank your trailer, emptying both hoppers on full noise, and send you on your way in just over a minute flat. It is worth noting that at some elevators you could only open one hatch at a time, and sometimes not all the way at once. That elevator could handle a high volume at high speed. Even someone who wasn't a custom harvest crew member could take one look at that place and appreciate the sophistication of it.

Overnight it rained cats and dogs. In the morning it was clear we wouldn't be idling up any time soon. I strolled up one block for my French vanilla coffee and headed a few meters down the road to the town's museum. It stretched over several buildings and had a zany, yet informative selection of exhibits. It covered old times in Regent, the local social and sporting history of the city, and former North Dakota Congressman and Senator Byron Dorgan, who was raised in Regent. I spent a good while browsing the section dedicated to Mr Dorgan. It had been assembled over some time. Its material covered several political eras. As well as enjoying a lengthy career, Mr Dorgan certainly had a knack for scoring some pretty memorable photo ops. As a former political employee and someone who had followed U.S. politics for a long time, I found it very engaging.

In the afternoon the word was given: we had been granted leave to head up to Dickinson, ND. Just over fifty minutes north of Regent, Dickinson is a service city that's home to around 20,000 people. It's spread-out, flat, and has lots of truck, diesel and machinery shops.

I liked it from the minute we drove in. We heard Dickinson was susceptible to what was happening with the price of oil. When the going was good, it was happy times all round. When the going wasn't so good, things could start to look grim. The other negative, for me at least, was how cold it would get. I do not function well in cold weather. The guys told me there's Midwestern cold, and a special breed of Midwestern cold that's found in North Dakota. I was sure that with a cup of Starbucks and a Carhartt jacket I would get by.

We called into a truck shop to collect some Kenworth parts. Before venturing inside we had a look at some customised oilfield trucks on the lot. We Snapchatted them to our friends around the world. Inside the shop, behind the counter, I noticed an Automann cap. It was fabulous. The cap was jet black and thick-billed. It had a blue trim and a United States flag embroidered on one side. I asked the man at the counter for the hat so I could buy it. He said, "No."

Taken aback, I thought 'Oh man, that hat is sweet.'

Then he said: "It's free, here, have it!"

The hat was that good I offered to pay for it. My collection of hats, at that time, numbered about thirty. That one stood out to me like a 'breaking news' headline banner on a website. I gratefully accepted the free hat and bought some chocolate to at least walk out of there having contributed in some way. Thank you, Wallwork Truck Center, for your generosity. You guys are awesome!

Supper was Buffalo Wild Wings. That restaurant chain was a point of division in the crew. Some of us liked Buffalo Wild Wings. Others were less enthusiastic. I was down with the place. The Offspring was playing when we walked in—that did not dim my enthusiasm for the franchise. I commented to the staff member on his outstanding choice of music. He thanked me and later admitted the playlist chose it randomly. We ordered up, chatted away, and had ourselves a real good time. As much as I enjoyed our meals out in the United States, it didn't change the fact that I've never had much of a sweet tooth. Stateside restaurant desserts were generally a bit much for me. In place of a restaurant dessert, if there wasn't a Dairy Queen nearby, I would order a flat white from Starbucks. That was, to my knowledge, the only chain in the United States that would serve up that iconic, New Zealand-invented combination of milk and coffee.

As was custom, we called in at the local Runnings to check it out. Kelvin and I held AR-15 rifles, shotguns, pistols, and spent a good while going through the gun section. We didn't see any bad Runnings stores in the Midwest. I have to say, that one up at Dickinson was really good. We browsed a while before we strolled on to the nearby Boot Barn. I had a chat to the girl there. A nursing student, apparently. Whether the uniform existed or not, we didn't know. I wanted to believe it did. I'm pretty sure the others did, too.

A short time later, the durum wheat was ready. We fired up our machines and pushed ahead. I would describe the fields we cut as very 'North Dakotan'; they all had at least some slope either in the field we were in or right nearby. There were always large blocks of trees visible. At the end of one field sat a large lake. It was a pretty sight. The farmer could've easily cashed in their check and sold that field on if they wanted to. They could have built some sort of hunting or resort lodge out of big lumber, complete with balconies and hot tubs, a bar stocked with whiskey and wine, and a steak-serving restaurant—the view north really was that good.

As soon as I woke up the next morning I scrambled to open my phone and look at the score from back home. Finally, we'd done it! After twenty years in the competition, the Hurricanes had won a Super Rugby title. Even though I was a long way from New Zealand rugby country, I was over the moon. The Hurricanes had made the Super Rugby final the year before. I'd gone to see it with Dad, only to witness a loss in the dying moments of the game—to the Highlanders, of all teams. All bitterness was forgotten that morning. I couldn't be happier my team had come out ahead of the rest. Long live the Hurricanes!

The new field we were cutting had a couple of nasty slopes. Rob had cut that field before so we knew it was safe. Still, I was wary of the slopes and how dodgy they looked. Kelvin had the job of tackling some of the uglier inclines. I radioed him and suggested we could time the unloading at the bottom so he didn't have to perform his Evel Knievel act going up the other side with any weight on. I was mighty careful where and how I turned, as it's wise to do with 54,000 lbs in the cart behind you. I played my part that day with the tractor and cart on all twelve wheels. At one end of the field there was a makeshift car dump; it was a pit which looked like an old duck pond or dugout, filled to the gunnels with hoary old automobiles. The messages and comments flew around the crew. Some contributions were wittier than others.

By 5 pm we were all out of wheat to cut. For some reason that day we only had one pickup to take personnel back to the staging area a few miles away. There was one place short for the ride back. I volunteered to wait it out for a bit until a return vehicle arrived. I lay down in the grass by the road and rested my boots on a lump of dirt. I stared out at the horizon. In minutes I drifted off thinking about life in general and what was next. What was ahead in six months? A year? A decade? I snapped out of it and reminded myself—there's nothing that can be done about it right now, so why bother? The only decision that needed to be made then and there was what beer I'd start with after knock-off. Within an hour I was in the pub, and—surprise, surprise—I found Cassie and the rock music guy there and into it. We weren't going early the next morning, so I joined in. I chose Bud Light and repeated that choice several times throughout the evening.

The next few days saw changeable weather and periods of downtime and maintenance. We washed our gear. The mechanics changed oil and filters. We blew off radiators, blew out filters, cleaned cabs, and greased everything that needed to be greased. With no harvesting in sight for a day or two, we got a heck of a lot done in a fairly short time. The weather did leave a chink in its armour one Wednesday afternoon. We quit our crew film screening and headed out to the field.

By that time in the season I'd learned to get through an Eaton Fuller 18-speed truck gearbox. When we washed the trucks in the days prior, I asked a couple of our trucking boys if I could have a shot in one of the Kenworth T800s in a safe area. They let me. It went well. I had watched Jake, Cory, George, Kelvin, John, Clint, Helmer, Cassie, Devin, and others make their way up and down through gears when I rode with them in the trucks. It did look challenging to me. But I still really wanted a go. Barely into Harvest 2016, I had made it one of my life's goals to drive a heavy diesel vehicle fitted with an engine brake, and to use that engine brake!

Operating an 18-speed gearbox isn't rocket science. Nor is it something everyone picks up in ten minutes, either. A good, grind-free shift up and down through the gears takes skill. Out in the field, one of the service trucks needed to be moved about 200 yards over to the edge of another field when it was done with refuelling. I felt somewhat cool when I volunteered and managed to do it smoothly, complete with a small engine brake sound-off to bring the vehicle to a safe and steady halt. I got a few eye-rolls and sly smiles from a couple of crew members who told me "we heard that, Paul". Barely a couple of hours later, a storm broke out. The thunder was so loud it sounded like a giant, God-like creature hitting metal with a hammer. That was us for the night.

Because pretty much everything with an engine bigger than 6.7 liters was washed clean, all that remained were the cars and the two pickups. We washed them down in the morning and headed on up to Dickinson again. A few guys had errands to run. I joined in because I knew it would only be a matter of time before we wound up at a machinery dealership of some kind, and because I had an errand of my own to run at the nearest Dairy Queen outlet.

We were rolling along Interstate 94 when I saw it—a tall, metal column with a Peterbilt sign on top. When I pointed it out, the crew members in the car with me reacted like parents might when their child spots a McDonald's sign right after the parents say "we should stop for food somewhere". Everyone in the car agreed: we should exit the highway and investigate the Peterbilt site immediately. Inside, I spent far too long eyeing up the hats and accessories cabinet. The guy behind the counter grew a little impatient. It showed. I would've too, if I'd watched someone take as long as I did. Eventually, I settled on a classic, navy blue Peterbilt logo hat, complete with a United States flag on the back. Pretty much everyone on the crew had work hats and travel hats. Work hats were often a brand of choice, such as John Deere or Case IH, and were worn with pride. But in our line of work, a 'work' hat would look new and tidy for all of about ten minutes. 'Travel' or 'going out' hats were only worn once or twice a month and were kept tidy. My new Peterbilt hat became one of my 'going out' hats on the spot. To this day, it's still one of them.

Close to Allstate Peterbilt of Dickinson lay Butler Machinery Company, a Caterpillar dealership. As I recall, we managed to pick up a couple of filters and other everyday parts from Butler. The real attraction, however, was right outside. We saw swathers, Caterpillar tractors—they're not something you run into every day—and, to the delight of Helmer, a pair of Gleaner combine harvesters. We took our time to climb in and on the machines. The Butler site reminded me to be grateful for just how many big bits of farm equipment I'd had a shot on over the past few months. There are very few, if any, other areas on the planet you can see such a variety of heavy, eye-wateringly expensive farm machinery like that all in one place. And the best bit? There was a lot more to come.

One the way back, during a typical crew Walmart stop, we saw the folks from Frederick Harvesting getting some shopping done. Even though we were in North Dakotan wheat country, it could not have been more obvious that we were looking at a group of custom harvesters. The light blue jeans, slim t-shirts, tractor caps, and hol-stered wrenches and pliers gave the game away in seconds.

As I strolled around Walmart to grab my fruit and popcorn snacks for the tractor, I couldn't help but think about how I liked the feel of Dickinson. I could picture my residence already. Fort Savage. In the garage would sit a diesel pickup and a Jeep Grand Cherokee to go with it. A dark-colored Mercedes-Benz SL500 would be parked up nearby. The garage would have an all-weather servicing area, and ample room for the three automobiles and the motocross bikes. At least a couple of the bikes would be two-strokes, of course. I'd have a mini-ramp and a couple of rails. Perfect for a warm-weather skateboarding session. Out the back I'd have ropes, a bag, and pads. Kickboxing workouts and sparring would take place. My wardrobe would be over-run with Carhartt and John Deere-branded hoodies and hats. It all sounded possible, as long as my house had an effective heating system.

When we got back to Regent, I called up an old high school buddy who was living in Reno, Nevada, where he was running the show at a place called RedRock Bar. We had a good old catch-up. As I gathered, Nevada could be a hot, arid, and unforgiving sort of place. At that time, I'd never been there before, so I was interested in Rhys's accounts of life in The Silver State. Living there certainly hadn't diluted his New Zealand accent, that was for sure. If you're by Reno sometime, drop by RedRock and pay him a visit! The beer's good, too!

At breakfast the next morning we had no further instructions. I stole away for a quick French vanilla and read my Frederick Forsyth book. Rob came to the trailer and told us to saddle up for an early afternoon start. We tried. It was a bit too wet. We sat, and I read for four hours before venturing out once more. The moisture was only *just* right, but that was good enough. We fired up and got rolling. A Green Day song played on the radio. I liked it, but I didn't recognise it. I would have described it as old-style Green Day. When the song finished, it became apparent why I didn't know it. The song had apparently just been released. I thought Green Day had done a good job with its new 'Bang Bang' track.

We roaded north and tackled a new section. The crop wasn't quite ready, and the dark cloud that was threatening us from the south didn't help things. Sue made us a hearty meatloaf dish that evening. It went down a treat. Right after supper, Tommy announced he was going to play *Top Gun* as the evening's movie. I made a quick dash to the vending machine—about 200 feet away, up on the main road—for an ice-cold can of my American treat, Diet Mountain Dew. The sugar content of a regular can of soda pop would cause my system to have a fit, so the sugar-free variety became a routine treat during my Harvest 2016. I returned just in time to get a good seat on the couch for a viewing of that film I never get sick of watching.

No-one woke us the next morning. We took advantage of the welcome sleep-in. I then recalled that a day earlier I'd seen the 'Low

Washer Fluid' indicator lights appear on both the Dodge pickups. I zipped up to the store and grabbed a gallon of the stuff for about three dollars and topped up the vehicles in need. Meanwhile, Tony and a couple of the crew went to check the wheat section. It was a no-go. I continued to read Frederick Forsyth's *The Afghan* that afternoon. In the evening we learned that Devin was on his way. He was headed to a dairy farm in the northern reaches of California. As much as we were happy he was going on to something he really wanted to do, we knew we'd miss him. I certainly would. Devin is a good sort. I have since enjoyed many a phone chat and catch-up with him, and I hope there are many more in the years to come. Lekker, boet!

I joined three others on the couch that evening for a meme session. We'd pull out our phones and share memes on a particular subject or in-joke that was going around. We all came close to bursting a rib with laughter that evening with the tasteless brand of humor we'd honed throughout the season. Not everyone would understand it. When you're together with the same bunch of guys for half a year, working hard, playing hard, and having a good time along the way, the jokes and gags only get better as the time goes on.

Later that evening, we got word the next crop would not be ready for a couple of days. Cory came by and asked if anyone else wanted to head down to Sturgis. I had no idea who, what, or where Sturgis was. I just said: "Yeah, I'm down!" I quickly learned from the Tennessee boys that Sturgis was a world-famous biker rally in South Dakota. It was an enormous gathering known for Jack Daniel's, leather, hard rock music, Vietnam veterans, and Budweiser. That night as I went to sleep, I wondered what I'd signed up for. As far as I was concerned, it was another adventure to be had. And, for me, any excuse to go to South Dakota was a good excuse.

Sturgis, South Dakota

August 2016

At 0600 we hit the road and headed south. The Sturgis-bound crew was Cory, Helmer, Philipp, Jake, Tommy, Kelvin, and me. The highway out of North Dakota showed us another side of the state. The further we went, the more barren the fields appeared. The hills got steeper. The growth was browner. As we pushed further south we found ourselves surrounded by a landscape which was similar to the Desert Road, a section of State Highway 1 that runs through a group of mountains in the central North Island of New Zealand. About an hour out of Sturgis we pulled into a gas station for coffee and breakfast. It was filled with bikers. They didn't look like people to be messed with. That said, there was a distinct 'If you don't bother me, I won't bother you' vibe going around.

Sturgis really was something else. When the infamous biker rally isn't on, Sturgis is home to around 6,000 residents. It's located in western South Dakota, on the northern side of the Black Hills National Forest, about thirty minutes north of Rapid City, SD. When the rally is on, Sturgis will host some 500,000 attendees. We heard that in 2015, the number hit around 700,000 bikers. On the way in we saw concert venues in fields, massive bike park-ups, big trucks, and a whole lot more. I knew we'd well and truly reached the town when I saw what I think was a 1933 Ford coupe. It looked just like the one that's on the cover of the ZZ-Top album *Eliminator*. There were enormous Jack Daniel's signs, Budweiser banners, Harley-Davidson flags, and motorcycle brand patches all around. In the air was a feeling of controlled chaos and excess. I looked over at Kelvin as we found somewhere to park. Both our mutual expressions said: 'Wow. Just wow. This is going to be fun.'

It would take another book to write down everything we saw, rode, tasted, sampled, checked out, and experienced at Sturgis. One of the best parts about our Sturgis excursion was that it came completely out of the blue. When I travelled to the United States I knew it was pretty likely I would see things like Mount Rushmore, the Midwestern plains, and the John Deere factory at Waterloo, Iowa. Surprisingly, I hadn't included a notorious biker rally on my to-do list. The outing to Sturgis was a sensory and cultural overload. It was a bold, underlined definition of Americana. If you'd asked me a week before our trip south if I knew about Sturgis, I'd have probably said: "Sturgis? Never heard of them."

At Sturgis it would have been rude not to order a Jack Daniel's to cool off with. I found one pretty quickly and sipped it back as I took in the sights. Nearby there were a few V8 motorcycles. They looked like something out of a Batman movie. Their guards and fenders angled off, sharply. They were painted blades, ready to slice open or intimidate anyone who got too close on the highway. The man who was selling these power-wielding beasts started one up and revved it hard. We'd have gone deaf in minutes if he'd kept that throttle pinned. We even got to sit on them for Facebook photos and Snapchats.

Every motorcycle company you could name probably had a stall or booth that day. We watched stunt performers shred rubber and risk life and limb performing burnouts, wheelies, and all kinds of tricks at high speed in small spaces. Philipp hit up the Harley-Davidson zone. We noted he was taking a while. Then we saw him, grinning ear to ear, in full riding equipment. We quickly put two and two together and worked out he'd talked his way into test riding a Harley—not only down the road, but out on the highway and up through the hills. Philipp took off and blasted down the tarmac like he was trying to put a piston through the top end of the machine. We smiled, shook our heads, and thought 'only Philipp'. He returned about twenty minutes later, beaming with pride. Good show, Philipp!

A text from North Dakota advised the wheat was still about forty-eight hours off. Cory suggested we make a night of it and head to Rapid City. It took all of about five seconds for a unanimous 'yes' vote from the crew present. Our democracy worked fast. Furthermore, the next day, we'd get a chance to go and see Mount Rushmore. We found accommodation near town and headed out for supper at the Firehouse Brewing Company, a craft beer and restaurant joint. I got an average-tasting brew. I've never cared much for craft beer. I ordered ground buffalo for supper. It could be served up for an extra two dollars in place of ground beef. To me, it tasted somewhere in between venison and beef. After that, we caught a screening of the recently-released *Bad Moms* flick. We all had a good laugh.

I woke up feeling a bit crook the next morning. I blamed it on the craft beer, even though I only had one. We called into Walgreens for some healing potions. Walgreens, a major pharmacy chain, sold alcohol and ice cream. I thought that was awesome. There are times in life where a few rounds of hard liquor, some ice cream, and a TV series binge are exactly what is needed. Walgreens can take care of all that. I picked up some Tylenol and Airborne before we hit the road for Mount Rushmore.

The road north to Mount Rushmore is worth doing in itself. It's winding, tree-lined, and truly breathtaking. It really is just like what you see on TV and in the movies. The weather wasn't too hot, and there was no sign of overcast conditions or rain on the way. At the entrance to Mount Rushmore we only had to pay about fifteen dollars per car to get in. Given it's one of the more well-known tourist destinations in the United States, if not the world, I thought that price was very reasonable. We grabbed a spot in the underground carpark. In the United States, most vehicle licence plates are emblazoned with unique graphics and colors from their states of origin; we saw examples from as far away as Maine and Florida.

Mount Rushmore is a treat. The viewing and catering areas are roomy, well laid-out, and can adequately see to a lot of people at once. We took our photos and marvelled at the hillside cut-outs of the four former Presidents' heads. We took the forest walk around the base of the sculpture and into the history room where you can read about and see how it was all put together. It was clear: the workers, planners and designers had done a heck of a job. On the way out we sampled what was sold as a former President's 'special blend' of ice cream. Whether or not that part was true, we didn't care. The ice cream was tops. I could've spent a whole day at Mount Rushmore. I would recommend it to anyone. It's a must-do. I remain thankful that I got the chance to see and experience it all with my friends.

Next to Box Elder, just out of Rapid City, sits Ellsworth Air Force Base. Ellsworth is home to the 28th Bomb Wing, a unit that operates the Rockwell B-1B Lancer bomber. Outside the base is the South Dakota Air and Space Museum, a free-entry attraction open to the public. I begged Cory for an hour to shoot out there and have a look. The group caught wind of it and said they'd all be keen to see it as well, much to my delight. A lot of the museum's interior content focused on the Cold War period. It features a number of nuclear-focused exhibits, namely shelters and missiles. Outside, there are several aircraft permanently sat there. The real treats were a B-1B and B-52, both of which you can walk right up to. Unless you are in the right place at the right time, or in the U.S. military, your chances of seeing one up close are slim. We had a good look around and left with some fond memories and brag-able photos. Cory didn't need to let us see that place on the way back. He could've called it a day and fast-tracked our trip back north. But he didn't. I'll always be grateful for that.

Regent, North Dakota

August 2016

I'd almost finished my Frederick Forsyth novel the next morning when Rob came in to ask for a grain cart operator and two combine boys. He'd do that when we were going to perform a test-cut. It was easier than rounding up the whole crew to fire up machines and move to a field that might not be ready. I volunteered and grabbed my water and food. The wheat in the new field went fine, although the weather pattern was a little interesting. Right over my tractor, without warning, the heavens opened and absolutely soaked my machine.

I looked around at Rob's combine. He was ticking along, dry as a bone. The others were too. I radioed other operators in the field and asked if they were getting wet also. They responded, "Um, no, what?" They must've looked over and seen the rainfall's selective targeting of machines. Apart from messing up my windshield, it didn't affect our operation that afternoon. The wheat cutting hummed along without event for the next couple of days. The fields had cambers and curves. I'd learned how to handle those in Kansas, of all places. I didn't always find it easy, but I reckon I got them done just fine. It was good to mix up the rhythm.

It only took another day or two to smash out the final few acres. After that, we cleaned and readied machines to head north for the border. When we were washing, right by the side road, a local contemporary stopped by and came over to chat. Then he asked if we wanted to see his new gun. "Sure," we said. It was a mean-looking 1911—not a Colt, though—complete with a holographic sight and a magazine loaded with the infamous .45 ACP hollow-point rounds. He removed the mag, checked the chamber was empty and handed me the weapon to examine. I didn't think anyone was going to try and jack him in a hurry. The next day and a bit were filled with washing down machines and loading them onto the trailers. It paid to have your gear spick and span when crossing borders, particularly international ones. We had those Case IH combines looking like they'd just rolled off the assembly line at Grand Island, NE.

Indian Head, Saskatchewan, Canada

September 2016

The morning had come. We were off to Canada! I didn't really know a lot about where we were going, except that it was really flat, sparsely populated, and the fields were meant to be enormous. I'd held on to this stereotype of rural Canadians as tall, broad personalities with long hair and beards. I imagined they wore beanies with maple leaves on them, rode snowmobiles, and listened to rock music while holding metal coffee flasks. Those simplistic images aside, I had no idea what we were in for. On the way to the United States–Canada border, we passed through Minot, ND, and went right by the front entrance of the nearby Air Force base. There was enough firepower over there to permanently rearrange a lot of the world's dirt and change the course of history in minutes. It felt a little eerie to drive past, knowing just what was around.

The United States–Canada border crossing was pretty relaxed. I presented my permit and passport, shut off the car, and answered the usual questions you might expect. Kelvin, Tony and I got an easy ride through. My guess was it was our passports and citizenship from Commonwealth nations and Britain. As relaxed as the Canadian border patrol staff were, I had no doubt they had some sort of hidden technology at work to see if you were lying about carrying contraband like drugs, forbidden weapons, and other items you were advised not to bring into Canada. We trekked through Manitoba for a short while before crossing provinces into Saskatchewan and stopping at Carnduff for the night. We found a top-end ice cream store across the train tracks. There was also a nearby gas station—key for grabbing that caffeine fix before hitting the road.

I got up a little earlier in the morning to fetch some coffee before we headed off. Like the journeys out of Minnesota and through Oklahoma into Kansas, I didn't know when we'd be stopping next, so it was smart to cull fifteen minutes of sleep in order to secure a breakfast wrap and a nice cup of coffee. The coffee was a tad more expensive in Canada. The plus, however, was that the milk was rich and fresh. In the United States we did not always have fresh milk as an option. Not so up in Canada! Another bonus was using the Canadian dollar. One Canadian dollar was pretty close to a New Zealand dollar at the time, so mental conversions were that much easier. Although, by that time, I was used to thinking in U.S. dollars. In Canada, the road signs had kilometres on them. Measurements were metric, and temperatures were measured in degrees Celsius. Some familiarity again. Sweet.

About forty minutes after leaving Carnduff we pulled into a truck stop for breakfast. I took a minute to have a look around the joint. Soon I found a Tim Hortons iced coffee. I'd heard about that name being synonymous with Canada. I grabbed one, as well as an Oreo brownie I'd never seen before. Neither item would do my system any good. I couldn't care less. We were firmly in adventure and discovery mode. It was my first time in Canada, just as it was for most of the American boys on our crew.

The caffeine had well and truly kicked in by the time we reached Indian Head, a small farming town on the Trans-Canada Highway. It's about an hour's drive from Regina, Saskatchewan's provincial capital. Clint and I went about readying our crew trailer. This time, we really were in a trailer park. It was all good; conveniently located about a five-minute drive from the farm, and within walking distance of the local shops and the pub. Being so close to town, as well as the farm where we'd work, was not something we took for granted.

After we'd readied our mobile home, Sue took us up the road to the farm, an outfit just north of Indian Head. It was an impressive, family-run setup. It had a bunch of storage bins, lots of New Holland machinery, Peterbilt trucks, immaculate grounds, some sweet Ford and GMC pickup trucks, a neat-looking tracked skid-steer, and a friendly dog named Lucy. The weather was mild. There were trees and bodies of water all around. All the people were friendly. They also said 'eh' a lot, to end sentences. Yeah, it was Canada alright!

Because my cart hadn't made it north yet, I spent a day operating the wheat bagging machine. It's a contraption that transfers wheat into a long, rubbish-bag-like wrap. The bagging machine was attached to a small New Holland tractor. At the 'bag' we met Ryan, a leading hand and machinery operator who'd done some time in the oilfields, and Bob, a full-time employee of the farm. Ryan and Bob were welcoming, laid-back, and gave us a run-down of what was going on that harvest. Ryan drove this awesome Ford F-series pickup truck that had about a mile of ground clearance. It tackled the field approaches with ease. Above us, the sky was a smoky haze. As Canadian as the farm seemed to me, that overhanging haze was not what I had in mind for an image of rural Saskatchewan. I asked

Ryan about it. He informed me it was in fact smoke from one of several forest fires to the south.

I joined Clint for fuel duty the next morning. My cart was due to arrive later that afternoon. Until then, it was back to bagging duty. Every grain farm worker or custom harvesting crew member knows that getting the bag to come out dead straight is a lot easier said than done. The tractor we had, while modern and steady, was articulated. When you're moving slowly, keeping any articulated machinery dead straight is a little more difficult than doing so with a rigid alternative. We experimented with a number of methods. We tried guide ropes, foot lines, and a jerry can in the distance to try and keep the bag line straight. John, our Jack of all trades, was one of several who had a go. He threw out the straightest line of all. By late afternoon I was back on my cart. I found the local rock radio station. It was called The Wolf, and the first song I heard was 'Limelight' by Rush. How Canadian!

The next morning it was cold and foggy. Before long, the rain set in. At breakfast time I remember sucking in cool air. I hadn't had a full winter since Wellington, New Zealand in 2015. It isn't 'North America' cold back there, but it's pretty chilly by Kiwi standards. That Saskatchewan morning was the first time I'd taken in air that cool for a long time. It was clear we weren't going to fire up any machinery that day. We took to the town, Indian Head, for a stroll around. I bought a café coffee. It was half-decent in flavor. In strength, it was weaker than a one-liter engine dropped in a pickup. I ended up shopping at a book sale in the library. I left with a Paul Garrison novel to keep me busy in my downtime.

After the next morning's breakfast, Rob said he needed a volunteer grain cart operator to go and help cut some lentils. I volunteered and headed out with him in the pickup. He dropped me at my cart, got into his combine, and we travelled a few miles along the grid roads to the field of lentils. To my untrained eye, they looked kind of like soybeans. They sat low and drooped. They were a tan, rusty color. The lentils cut relatively slowly and went through the combine easily. I worked on them with Rob for about an hour. The field had some dips and undulations and went around a corner by a shed and a block of trees. Anything other than dead flat seemed somewhat unusual for that corner of Saskatchewan. It rivalled Kansas in being about as hilly as a marble benchtop.

While I waited for Rob's combine to fill up, I ventured over to the next field to meet some of the in-house farm crew. A young bloke climbed out of his tractor, wandered over to me and said, "Hey mate, how's it going?" He had an Australian accent thicker than the steel on the Sydney Harbour Bridge. Even as a Kiwi, hearing that on the other side of the world instantly takes you back to the Southern Hemisphere. The friendly Aussie was Ben, a sparky and all-round farm machinery operator from mid-Queensland. He offered me a jam in his tracked New Holland T9 tractor and grain cart. I looked over and saw Rob's combine flashing in the distance. If I'd had another few minutes I'd have gratefully had a run on the blue monster machine. On instruction, I unloaded my lentils into a farm-owned Peterbilt truck and headed over to link up with Rob.

In the lentils field, Rob and I made our way towards a Quonset farm shed. Rob radioed me: "Paul, park up. Go over to that shed and take a look. Tell me what you see in there." There was something odd about the way Rob said it. He was relaxed, for one, and almost sounded like he was about to tell a joke. I didn't know what to make of it. Nonetheless, I did as I was told. Rob was about 300 feet off, combining away in the lentils. Over at the shed it was dead quiet. There was no-one around. But something just felt … off. I yanked at the door but it wouldn't open. I could've sworn I heard a noise from inside the shed. I drew my knife, flicked the blade open and concealed it in my Swanndri jacket sleeve. I yanked harder at the door and it railed open. I was expecting Tommy, Clint, or one of the other crew members to leap out of nowhere and scare the hell out of me. No-one did. I don't know why I drew my blade. I would never have deployed it against one of our own. I guess it lowered my heart rate a bit.

I went back to the tractor, idled up and radioed Rob. "Copy, Rob," I said.

"Yeah," he said.

"Rob, there's half a dozen of what I believe are canola pickup headers. They're strapped down on flat-bed semi-trailers. They're a bit dusty, but they look in pretty good nick," I confirmed.

"Good, that's what should be in there," came the reply.

I laughed at the relief I felt. I genuinely thought I was about to fall victim to some juvenile scare prank. I can be highly strung at times; the team knew it. I am someone who is prone to getting a fright. But, to be fair, if someone else said they were going to orchestrate a similar prank at the expense of another crew member, I'd have gladly volunteered and got in on it.

Come morning, the wheat was good. Right back to it. We headed to a lengthy, rectangular-shaped field. It was dead flat and had a couple of old structures that were accurately described as haunted houses. They looked creepy, yet perversely inviting. With the old, ailing wooden houses and the crop surrounding them, the whole scene reminded me of the *All Hope is Gone* album cover art by Slipknot.

Because our truck drivers didn't have a very long run back to the farm's own wheat bins and bag machines, they would sometimes have a few minutes to wait around. Tennessee Jake rode with me in the cart and had himself a real good time. He would take over the controls and operate the thing better than I could. Jake had a knack for anything related to farm machinery and tended to pick it up very quickly. I was always happy to let him have a run himself. Supper that evening was Sue's signature tater tots, corn, and mince dish. It tasted great, and I'm fairly certain it was a crew-wide favorite.

When our field of haunted houses was done we roaded out towards a place called Sintaluta. As we traveled the grid roads to get there, we were treated to some fantastic local views. When you're a couple of meters off the ground you can see quite a bit out the window. On the way, we saw a vandalised road sign with a very rude word written on it. How un-Canadian! We queried each other on the radio to confirm, through suppressed laughter and disbelief, what we'd just seen. Tony suggested that a couple of English custom harvest workers in the area were the prime suspects!

We arrived at the field and drove in via a sloping road. It was sort of like a track towards a decline or portal entry at a mine site. Right next to it was something of a makeshift motocross track. I'd have given a lot to have had my bike with me then. It looked awesome. The wheat field was an obstacle course in itself. It had corners, dips, rises, trees, and several different sections. A couple of contracted B-train trucks arrived to help us with grain haulage back to the farm. One of them, on the way into the field for a couple of runs, must've broken the land-speed record for a double-trailer-hauling Peterbilt in a wheat field. I'd seen big rig trucks move slower than that on the open highway.

We looked on in humor, apprehension, and disbelief as the driver tried to break the sound barrier on his way into the field. Because those two trucks weren't numbered like ours, Tony and I had to find a way of identifying which was which. We went by drivers instead. We narrowed it down to 'the guy who looks like Tom Clancy' and 'the other guy', at my suggestion. It was heart-warming to hear the crew agree with my description of the driver who looked so much like the late author. If he'd worn a USS Iowa BB-61 cap and a pair of those smoked lens glasses, he could've fooled almost anyone.

Another morning, another day slowed down by troublesome moisture. As per standard procedure, we immediately set out about greasing up. My windscreen and filters had taken a real hiding. They were in dire need of a clean-up. The Wolf radio station announced it had a Green Day song coming up next. Tony, a fellow Green Day fan, leaned out his cab door and signalled me. I signalled back: yes, I'd heard it too. I told him I hoped it was 'When I Come Around'. It was. To add to our morning's entertainment, we saw a bright yellow, day-cab Peterbilt approaching the intersection next to the field. More accurately, we heard it coming a quarter mile away. Its straight pipes threw out a deafening, clattering tone of engine braking noise. It was as if the driver purposely loaded the engine just a touch more so the Jakes sang that little bit louder. Almost everyone in the crew later commented on "that big yellow Pete" downshifting at the intersection that morning. We were all fans.

Our new field was right next to a cliff with a drop-off of a few hundred feet. The land down below was green, rugged, and had a big river flowing through it, just like the Rangitikei district back home. There was a surplus of truck drivers that afternoon so I invited Jake to roll in the cab again. He'd always make the time go quicker, and it was good to have a quick breather while he blasted around at the controls. Combine operators had the luxury of the GPS-driven autosteer function. Grain cart operators didn't! When he was done, Jake made his way into a combine. I saw him leave my machine, so I assumed he'd gone to stretch his legs and head back to his truck. I only noticed he'd taken the controls of a combine when

I was unloading it. I was forced to do a double-take as I observed the operator's apparently sudden change in appearance.

"We're going on a road trip." Those were Rob's words at breakfast time the next morning. We readied our machines for 'road mode' and headed north on the highway. We saw some nice-looking houses above the shores of Katepwa Lake. They reminded me of some of the places that overlook New Zealand's enormous Lake Taupō. We continued along Saskatchewan Highway 56 and made our way up a steep, winding road that led us to a table-top plain, not far from the town of Balcarres. We passed a magnificent-looking old church, which apparently was built by volunteer labourers in the nineteenth century. The route in was aptly named 'Stone Church Road'. We found a staging area, got unloaded, and fired up to take on our new field.

The wheat yield was good. The setup was ideal. Although we were always moving, the timing worked out well. Tony and I could fit about three 'flashing' (three-quarter full) combine loads in each of our carts before it was ready to unload. We had a bit of a trek back to the bagging machine, maybe about a half mile or so, but if we kept a move on, we'd make it back to unload, turn around and head back just as the next three combines were filling up. I looked after three and he looked after three. We powered back and forth all day long without interruption.

A random two-way radio conversation about recent world history kicked off. Kelvin, Tony and I chipped in about the Commonwealth nations' link. Rob made a sarcastic, somewhat disparaging remark about the situation with his dry, sardonic brand of humor. It was an absolute pearler. It had the Commonwealth boys in stitches, although the joke was really at the expense of Australia and New Zealand. I cannot for the life of me remember exactly what Rob said, but I know we clearly saw the funny side of it. Up at the bagging machine, I saw what I thought was a dangerous snake. I was alarmed at first before I learned it was a virtually harmless Garter snake. I kept an eye out for it all day. We knocked over the entire section by nightfall and loaded headers in the dark. It was a long, tiring, but productive day.

The following days of harvesting passed by with few incidents. Tony's tractor and my tractor threw up engine filter and heat warnings because of the warm, dusty conditions. I'd kept an eye on the temperature. Nothing seemed out of sorts. Even though we'd blown out air and cab filters only days earlier, we had to do it all again so we could both get up and running. The tractors both fired into life with their newly-cleaned filters.

It was a cold, crappy morning at breakfast time. No harvesting would take place, and Jake needed some replacement glasses. Kelvin, Tommy and I decided to accompany him on a trip to Regina. We called the optometry outfit to ensure they didn't close before we got there. As Canadian as ever, they said, "Oh it's fine, we'll wait for you." On the way into Regina I felt like I was driving into the New Zealand city of Palmerston North. It was flat, surrounded by farmland, and it had a large industrial area with several machinery outlets. While Jake and Kelvin hit the optometrist, I sat with Tommy and listened to a couple of episodes of the Grunt Style series *Bedtime stories with 1st Sergeant*. They were as hair-raising and entertaining as ever. We hit a Walmart. It was just like what we would see in the United States, except there was a Tim Hortons out the front instead of a McDonald's. I purchased a copy of Queen's *Greatest Hits* album, a Hawk hoodie, and a hot cup of Tim's, eh!

We called by the Case IH dealership to pick up some pre-ordered parts so we could remedy a combine's manifold issue. There was another machinery yard nearby. We eyed up the gear and had a look inside it, just like we did on our expedition to Dickinson. Across town there was a Cabela's. We called in to see what the Canadian alternative was like compared to the United States. The prices were a little bit higher. Other than that, it wasn't much different. I left with a fishing hat for Dad. Cabela's gear isn't readily available in New Zealand, and my dad is a keen fly fisherman.

On the way out of town, we called into a John Deere dealership, South Country Equipment, at the coercion of me and Tommy. Inside, I checked out a late model tractor with Kelvin. I'd just climbed out of the cab when I stepped back to get a better look at the loader implement on the front. What I didn't see was the stack of pallets right behind me. The second my balance was upset, I shot my arm out behind me to stop the fall. I hit thin air. In that second I panicked. As a younger man, I skateboarded for several years. I did it for long enough to know when I was in danger of falling and landing on the back of my head. Such falls have killed skateboarders. I managed to twist my body and land on my upper back, right on the side of another pallet that was loaded with merchandise. It was wholly undignified. I went straight over backwards and took out part of a carefully-stacked store display in the process. It was obvious in a second I hadn't hurt myself. Kevin lost it. He roared with laughter. I got up and said: "See, I am head over heels for John Deere." Kelvin shook his head. I think I saw him smile as he walked off, still shaking his head.

Back in Indian Head, the crop wasn't quite ready. Rob and Sue had to dash into town for a half day. We looked up the local to-do list and found a paintball arena that would take us that afternoon. It was a good, fun way to let our hair down. We played several rounds of capture the flag, defend the fort, and at the end, 'empty the ammo'. We left tired, bruised and thoroughly entertained. On the outskirts of Indian Head lies an old-school style ice cream parlor. It had all kinds of soft-serve flavors. We sampled one each on the way back to top off a fun day out.

127

Onida, South Dakota, United States

September 2016

I enjoyed Canada. I learned a lot and had fun. But throughout Harvest 2016, the United States had become my home. When we headed back down, past the border, all the way to South Dakota, although I'd only 'lived' there a few weeks, it sure felt like a return to old turf. As soon as we arrived in Sully County, the recent memories flooded back. But summer was over and done with. It was time for the fall harvest. Sue called me and requested I take a detour via the Onida township and order a couple of pizzas to feed the crew. I rocked up, placed the order, and was told it would take a little while. As I waited, I hit the video poker machine and walked off a little richer. The few dollars I'd bet turned into several more. I used them to purchase S'mores ingredients for the crew later on. When I was done gambling, I collected the fresh pizzas and headed back to camp. It was right at the very spot we'd called home during the summer harvest. It was great to be back.

The truck-licensed crew members headed north the next morning to fetch the remainder of field equipment from our Canadian excursion. Back at camp we readied the on-hand equipment and prepared the machines for the fall crops we were about to harvest: corn and soybeans. Concaves were swapped, services were carried out and cabs were cleaned. That evening we were allowed to shoot down to Pierre for supper. Mad Mary's delivered the goods again. I took the radical step of not ordering a Bud Light. Instead, I sampled the Bud Light Lime. It was refreshing and excellent. Runnings had some well-priced Carhartt gear to get me through the colder weather. I knew it was about to get chilly outside. I spared no expense when I purchased a big jacket to keep me warm. I was more than happy to shell out a few extra bucks to stay toasty.

That evening I called Mum and Dad in New Zealand. As I spoke to them I saw some movement out the window of the truck I was sitting in, about fifty feet away. I thought it was either a large, well-fed domestic cat like a Maine Coon, or some kind of mountain lion. I kept trying to make out as much as I could in the dark without disturbing the creature. I relayed what I saw to Mum and Dad. They encouraged me to try and get a picture after the phone conversation was done. I tried to edge open the door as quietly as possible. The mysterious cat was spooked and made a run for it. I never saw anything like it again. During the rest of our time in Onida, I always wondered if that creature, whatever it was, would make another appearance in the dead of the night.

A day later we struck a blow for fall harvest. All our field machinery was back in the United States. We hit the soybeans over by Gettysburg. When you cut wheat, you don't have to run your combine in the exact same direction the crop is planted in. Not so with soybeans. Like corn, the soybeans need to be cut with the machine moving in the same direction and angle on which the crop was seeded. The combine's ground speed, and fan, concave and rotor settings need to be right on the button to avoid the machine shattering and cracking the beans, or throwing them straight out the back. I took all this in on the radio while making sure I was doing my best to get the cart driving right. It wasn't really a whole lot different to wheat. Maybe a little slower. The boys must've set the combines up right, because we plowed through those beans like there was no tomorrow. Even Rob commented at one section, "We're raising hell here."

The next morning's weather enveloped us in mist. We had a go at the crop, but the moisture level held us off. It was supposed to be ok in a few hours. We halted combines and tractors before we switched to hauling product to Lebanon, SD. I nominated myself as the day's 'scale boy' for something to do. It also meant a bit of walking around, which helped me stay warm. The weather had certainly begun to cool down. My debut as a scale boy was short-lived. By late afternoon we were cleared to start up again. We went at it until about eight that evening. Having Capital City Rock back on was a morale-lifting bonus. The only downer was right after I'd distributed that evening's suppers to the combines, I switched my FM radio on to hear Fuel's track 'Shimmer' half-way done. I was gutted I'd missed the intro; I really like that song. Capital City Rock also played 'Black Hole Sun' by Soundgarden, one I hadn't heard in a long time, and 'Good' by Better than Ezra. The station hadn't lost any form while we were away. After knock-off, I called Richard, a close friend of mine from my high school years at Wanganui Collegiate. He had since moved to Salt Spring Island, British Columbia, in Canada. I ran my recent adventures past him and had a good old catch-up.

Minot, North Dakota

September 2016

The rain absolutely hosed down. We heard it throughout the night knowing we could sleep longer. Sleep-ins are seldom taken for granted by a custom harvest crew member. We still had a few trucks left in North Dakota, near the Canada–United States border. A crew of four was needed: three truckers and one car driver. I was asked if I wanted to join the moving crew. I gladly accepted. A road trip anywhere meant seeing something new and at least a small adventure of some sort. I linked up with Cory, Kelvin, and Cassie for the journey. We had some relatively meaningful conversations on the way. Although it was just a regular trip to go an collect a few trucks, the rib-cracking comedy and eye-opening discussion on the way up made it all worthwhile.

I recognised Mound City, Linton, and other settlements on the way up. Cory played aloud a YouTube comedy routine that had us in constant stitches. I drove the final leg to Minot, a city of about 48,000 that's right up the top end of North Dakota. We'd also got another peek at the Minot Air Force Base, complete with the sign at the front gates that read: *Only The Best Come North.*

We called into Pizza Hut for supper. We were served by a young man who was a spitting image of a well-known Australian international and Queensland State of Origin rugby league football representative. I ran the comparison past Kelvin, a Queensland resident, who saw the likeness and laughed aloud. The internet told me there was a Dairy Queen nearby. I tracked it down. The Oreo Blizzard was a welcome treat before we set off. The motel for the night was a welcome change. In our trailer, we only had a few square meters of personal space per crew member. While a double bed and WiFi on demand was an everyday luxury for many, it meant a lot to us, even if it was only for a few hours.

Despite the good motel and comfortable bed, I slept poorly. Kelvin, on the other hand, had to be woken from his deep slumber. We made the most of the complimentary breakfast and headed north to the staging area to idle up the trucks and get ready to head straight back down state. I helped the truck drivers with their pre-trip inspections, taking on board as much information as I could.

Truck #3, driven by Kelvin, developed a bit of a heating issue on the way back. We called in to a gas station to inspect the radiator and surrounding areas, only to confirm the radiator wasn't too plugged, and there was not much we could do about it there and then. Kelvin adjusted his RPM to an optimal level to work the fan harder. The weather had cooled down even more, which helped. Had we been thrown that curve ball in the heat six weeks earlier, it might've been a different story.

Onida, South Dakota

September–October 2016

The inclement weather lifted. We were back in the soybean game. The new fields were bigger, longer, and relatively uninteresting. The beans made for a generally slower pace of harvesting. The weather transformed the landscape completely. The harvested wheat fields and low-hanging cloud gave me the impression we were in a different state altogether. I knew I was in my good old South Dakota. I was just appreciating it through a different lens. Despite the fog, cloud, and gloom, there was still quite a breeze blowing. It got so windy at one point that it moved the scale numbers on my cart around. That took some force!

Despite the whistling wind, we knocked over that section with ease. The crew was split in two for the next mission. I was grouped with George, Cassie, Kelvin, and Tommy. On the first morning with our new sub-crew, I ventured into town with the service truck driver to collect diesel from the M.G. Oil Company. I was wearing my hat, gloves, a thick layer on the skin, and a solid Carhartt jacket I'd picked up the week before at Runnings. At M.G. Oil that morning was Scott Brown, the owner of Brown Harvesting. He was holding a coffee and wearing a hooded sweatshirt. He looked at my layers of clothing and my body language that clearly signalled I was cold. He stared, oddly, for a moment. His expression said: 'Gee, it's not *that* cold, is it?' I think Scott and I probably had different understandings of what defined 'cold'.

The new fields were all rectangular. Two combines and one cart made for a leisurely, stress-free cut. I think we all enjoyed the slight change in pace. That evening we tuned in and listened to the first Presidential Candidates' debate. Throughout most of my life I had viewed and listened to American politics from New Zealand. It was fascinating to listen, live, to the broadcast from over in New York. Later that evening, Cassie brought out his metal coffee flask and discovered the contents to still be hot. He necked the coffee and proceeded to dance around the machines like he was at a Groove Armada concert. When he took off in his truck I asked him: "Cassie, are you doing alright there, bro?" His response was: "I am flying away like a witch on a broomstick!"

The next morning's start was a carbon copy of the previous day's. We fuelled up and got going on a big, long section. It was pretty cold in the earlier hours and proceeded to warm up to a more comfortable level as the day grew older. Even with two machines, it didn't take long to finish up and move on to the new field. It was *huge*. It had low points, corners and sections where you couldn't see the machines as they dipped and ducked away from my line of sight. I'd say it would've been one of the larger fields we tackled. At a guess, it would have been at least a full section (640 acres) in size. In fact, it was located not far from the monstrous wheat field we'd taken down in the summer cut.

We made a good dent in it before Sue brought us a Mexican supper, complete with a tasty burrito. I vividly recall the drive home that night. The route we took was as dusty as an old Western wagon trail. Even with a comfortable distance behind the vehicle in front, the dust and fog meant we could only see about twenty feet ahead. It was like driving into a continuous vortex that only ended and started again at intersections. The insects and dust gave it the appearance of a scene from a space-focused movie, a rocket ship blasting from one galaxy to another with the stars flying past. Except it was us at the controls and we certainly couldn't move too quickly.

The weather allowed another early start the next morning. The crop condition meant we did have to slow down a bit. That also meant the grain cart would spend much of its time with the engine switched off. I'd only collect beans from both machines at one end of the field so the combines could comfortably do a return trip without an excess load, and so the cart only had to be driven about 200 feet. We agreed on a role-swap; Cassie was appointed captain of the grain cart, and Kelvin let me take the controls of the combine. I'd sat in the combines with the guys on several occasions. Helmer, Kelvin, and Clint had all given me detailed running commentaries of what they were doing, at my request. By that point in the season I had enough knowledge built up that I was confident in having a crack at it myself. Kelvin watched me closely to ensure I didn't wreck anything or stray wayward. The hour or so combining I was given seemed like it took five minutes. I had a great time. I got Kelvin to Snapchat me at the wheel and send it to my cousins Phil, Tom, Rob, as well as others at home to confirm, yes, I got on a combine!

Day three on the 'big' field. We were joined by a fleet of John Deere combines harvesting the sunflowers next to us. I didn't even see them until one drove about 100 feet from me. There was no danger of a collision, but it sure did come out of nowhere and startle me for a moment. It was even flying a 'Jolly Roger' skull and crossbones pirate flag. It snuck up on me, just like an ominous pirate ship. It was neat to watch the sunflowers being taken down. The header was positioned a few feet off the ground, and the combine moved with some real ground speed on it. I would've guessed it was moving quicker than five miles per hour. I'd eaten my fair share of sunflower seeds by then, so I enjoyed watching how the product was brought in.

As we roaded back to camp that evening we saw another group of John Deere machines making a start on some corn. I managed to make eye contact with the grain cart operator. We looked at each other, nodded our caps, and flicked our lights. It was a sign of mutual respect. We both knew the highs and lows that came with each other's jobs. If that cart operator is one day reading this I am willing to bet he or she will recall that small but meaningful exchange. Before bedtime, we joined Cory for his nightly press-up routine. Cory had taken part in the twenty-two push-ups per day for twenty-two days challenge to raise awareness about suicides in the veteran community. Cory led us in double-count push-ups, meaning we would actually complete forty-four push ups instead of the standard, single-count twenty-two repetitions that most participants were doing. The video is still online, to my knowledge. I felt honored to be part of it.

Again, we had to give the beans a rest for a bit. That meant we were back to hauling corn kernels from the farm silos to a collection depot. I was assigned to 'handle duty' that day, turning the crank handle on the silo to control the flow of corn on to the auger so the trucks could be loaded. Although the bean harvest of the week before was not strenuous, the change of scene was good to break the rhythm. The direction of the wind and the position of the bin meant I didn't get too cold that day. Had the handle been in a different place, I'd have ended up walking a mile or so back and forth just to stay warm!

Later that day I rode along with Jake in his truck. It was a routine haul that ended up taking a hair-raising turn. On the way to the corn drop-off point in Onida you had to cross the train tracks. Trains frequented the line at that time of year. As we went to cross, we saw a locomotive, with carriages in tow, maybe four or five hundred feet away. As we looked out to the left, we saw the train aimed right for us. Jake stopped before the tracks. We both looked at the train and debated whether or not it was moving towards us.

Jake paused, looked again, and eased off the clutch to crawl forward over the tracks. The very moment he did, the train's front lights lit up and began to flash. The driver sounded the horn. It was already too late to back out. I yelled, "Go man, go, go!" Jake got a similar shock but calmly guided the semi-truck forward. We wondered if the driver was 'trolling' us and having a laugh. He or she would've seen us come to a complete stop, pause, and move forward. If we'd quit moving for a couple of minutes the train would have hit us, sure. But being at least 400 feet out, that wasn't likely. The sight of that train moving towards us, there, prone on the tracks, was not pretty. As we drove off, we roared with laughter, but it was really a nervous laughter that concealed a wish for something like that to never happen again.

When we got back to camp I suggested we do S'mores. A few guys grabbed a car and went on a quick firewood mission along the surrounding grid roads. The downed tree branches yielded plenty of wood. In no time at all we had enough, complete with an old metal box frame, to make a S'mores-suitable fireplace. To make a S'more you take two crackers, a marshmallow and a few squares of chocolate. With the crackers and chocolate ready, you roast the marshmallow on the fire, squash it between the crackers and chocolate, then take it down.

I'd seen S'mores in a film many years earlier. Although everyone was on board with the delicacy that was S'mores, I got the impression the practice of making them by the fire was a lot less widespread than I had imagined. I had pictured it as an American rite of passage that *everyone* did. I picked it was more common in the movies than in real life. Nonetheless, we all joined in and washed the sweet treats down with ice-cold beer. Looking back, that was one of our last nights all together as a crew socialising. It was just a good, relaxing, and fun time together.

Rob and Sue were back in Minnesota temporarily. That meant we were on our own for a few days. There were no beans ready to cut, so back to haul trucking it was. I helped where I could and moved the trucks in between positions in the yard. I enjoyed it. I relished every little bit of practice on the Road Ranger gearbox I could get. The guys even let me move a couple of trucks from the 'home' bins over to the yard. It was a trip of all of about 1,000 feet, but I still got a kick out of it. It required gear shifts. And, of course, I used the engine brakes. You know, just to make sure they worked properly.

Shain, the resident farmhand, and former crew member of the Holland outfit, came by to check out the auger one day. About a day or so earlier its exhaust system had split open. It sounded, as Helmer commented, like a motorbike. Fortunately, we had Clint, an Indiana-state-ranked welder, handy with the rods and equipment to fix the auger up again. Gone was the deafening rev. I spent the day climbing on top of trucks. I spotted for the drivers and guided them to move forward, stop, and go. It was repetitive, but the time went fairly quickly. When you're up there, clinging to a trailer, concentrating on your balance and, more importantly, not falling off, the time flies by. I was covered in corn dust from head to toe by the end of that day.

We loaded, hauled, and serviced for the next two days. When the corn was done, we took to washing down and vacuuming all vehicles at camp. Rob's pickup had its satellite radio intact. I remember we stumbled across a jazz channel, chuckled at it, and spent a relaxing afternoon detailing the vehicles while listening to the smooth tunes. The problem was, we forgot to change it back. A couple of days later, Rob climbed into the freshly detailed pickup with a few of us. When the radio came back on with 'Bring It' by Kim Waters blaring out, Rob queried, somewhat amused, who had chosen this particular music in the pickup and why. It was me and Jake. We both caught each other's glance and decided it was better to let the situation quickly die off rather than try and explain why, with the scores of channels available, we thought it was funny to put sensuous jazz music on the radio. When I was at the wheel I would typically tune Sirius to the Octane or Lithium rock music channels, or 80s on 8. Rob enjoyed the country music stations and 70s on 7. More so than the jazz, apparently.

The next morning it was unforgivingly cold. The puddles around camp were frozen. A number of taps wouldn't run because the water inside the pipes was rock solid. There was no harvesting that day. We worked on some header issues and carried out a bit of servicing out in the field instead. The corn was nearly ready to harvest. Because that corn would come into the combines so quickly, we would only need two of them in action. Rob and Tommy's machines would be the final two survivors. By that time we'd started cleaning down and loading the no-longer-needed machines so George could ferry them back to Minnesota.

When that day was done I went, on my own, and deleted a couple of bottles of Miller Chill. I sat, looking west, on the back of a header trailer in the rear machinery parking area. It was my kind-of-secret spot. I believe one or two other crew members knew about it, too. I don't think anyone revealed they knew about it in hope to keep it vaguely secret. It was a perfect place to watch the incredible South Dakota sunsets. Of the many things I would miss, I knew Midwest sunsets would be one of them. When I'd sit at that spot, I'd drink away with the knowledge harvest wasn't over. I would remind myself I should appreciate and enjoy the experience, right there, in the moment. When I return to Onida one day, I will go back to that very spot and enjoy a couple of cold ones.

The next morning, George had another machine ready to be taken back to Minnesota. His wife had come by to drop in and visit, and she'd ride along with George in the truck across the state line. I ferried them both out to the machine site the next morning. On the way, we discussed military service, civics, and college/university education in the United States versus New Zealand. On the way back I got word the corn harvest was about to kick off. I stopped by camp to grab my water and food, then made a beeline for the field. John had temporarily taken over my cart and had it flying around. Fortunately, I was allowed back on it to continue.

Corn harvesting is *quick*. We had two carts chasing two combines. Tony and I had those carts absolutely sailing around the field trying to keep up. With only two machines it was pretty easy to gauge who was where, as opposed to keeping tabs on six of them. Still, the big corn kernels would fill the combines' hoppers mighty fast. Also, like sunflowers, the combine harvesters' ground speed was significantly quicker than wheat. Corn was new to me. It was sort of like soybeans, but much quicker and with fewer machines. With several guys now off their combines, we had no shortage of truck drivers. Jake co-piloted the cart with me on several occasions and enjoyed coming along for the ride.

Into the night we soldiered on. We set upon a new section of corn. I remember it wasn't long before the next Presidential Candidates' debate was due to come on the radio. I also nearly managed to flip the tractor and cart. Rob had pushed over to the east end of the field and needed me for unloading so he could complete the headland— the area around the edge of the field—in one go. I rolled towards the field entrance and headed in the direction Rob had taken. I didn't realise, until it was almost too late, just how steep the rounded entry to the field on the contour bank was. I'd never seen the field up close before, and it was pitch black. Despite the strong spotlights, I completely misjudged the entry point's angle. To make it in, I'd have had to turn slightly to traverse the angle and not scrape the hell out of the bottom of the tractor.

I think if I'd attempted it, that would've been the end of that. My overly cautious approach to machinery operation might have been the only thing that saved me that night. I was maybe six feet from either flipping the tractor on its side or at least blowing out the welds, coupling, and the PTO, all in one go. Even in the dark, I managed to reverse around about teen feet on the angle and make my way in, about 200 feet further down. Rob understandably told me to hurry up and get down the east end. I responded, "Yep, on my way, be right there Rob." I thought it was better not to try and explain I'd possibly almost totalled his machine.

With a surplus of guys and an accident that'd smoked his ankle, Austrian Philipp was to be on his way. I drove him into Onida to bid farewell. I knew I'd miss Philipp's devious brand of humor. After the final drop-off, it was right back into the corn. The harvesting went by in a flash and the fields seemed to be over and done with before they began. In the trailer that night, with some spare data John gave me, I watched the *Doubt* documentary about the Smart/

Hope Marlborough Sounds disappearance that occurred nearly twenty years earlier in New Zealand. The documentary made me somewhat homesick—the unique New Zealand geography, police cars, and accents took me right home. About an hour after I stopped watching, I woke up from my sleep and went to grab a drink of water. For a second, when I woke, I thought I was back home again, not in the middle of a crop farm in the upper Midwest.

With Philipp gone, there were only six guys left in the crew trailer. It seemed a lot emptier not having him around. After a hot breakfast, we rolled back out to the section to keep knocking out the kernels. Rob's combine threw up an engine fault. The operation reduced to just me and Tommy while the problem was attended to. After Rob's machine was back to full functionality, he radioed us and asked who had a hunting knife on them and knew how to use it. Tony answered before I could, "Dare I ask why?" It turned out there was a dead deer in the field that needed taking care of. Tony and Cassie drew their blades and went to work to remedy the situation. We moved on to yet another long, rectangular section. Tommy said over the radio he thought the field runs, end to end, seemed longer at night. The general consensus was yes, they did appear longer in the darkness.

The following morning was a touch warmer. In my view, it was still cold. The two-cart, two-combine setup was working well and we had a quick rhythm going in no time. The corn was flying off the cob. The short run of only a couple of miles for trucks to the bins and back meant we never had to wait for an empty truck. Our field was particularly long. So long that, at some points, Rob would cut the corn on an angle with a teardrop pattern so us cart drivers could move alongside for an unload and turn around to head back the way we came in. The long, straight rows prompted calls on the radio that we were filming a remake of *Children of the Corn*. I still

142

hadn't seen that film, but I'd heard enough about it to picture what this new take might look like. Later in the afternoon, a lone Angus cattle beast wandered into the field. That was a rare sight in our area of South Dakota. We couldn't see a brand, but it was tagged and didn't appear lost or distressed. It soon disappeared into the hilly, grazing field south of our position without incident.

Out of nowhere, Rob came on to the radio with a small address to us. He ended it by saying it was scenes like these we would never forget the rest of our lives. I nodded to myself. Cassie jumped on to the radio and proclaimed he wanted to forget us all.

"Who pissed in your oatmeal this morning, Cassie?" Rob asked, humorously.

Cassie then shot back, "No Mr Holland I am only joking, I will never forget any of you, I want to remember it all forever." You could almost see and hear each crew member shaking his head and laughing. I'm sure, if she heard it on the two-way radio, Sue reacted the same way. It was a streak of humor that was endemic to the wild world of Cassie.

My diary description of the next morning was 'cold as sin'. I guess that was our crew's polar opposite to a very hot day, which we would have described as 'hot as *balls*'. I followed as the scout cart—the one at the front—with Rob and Tommy as they split the field in two and cut the headland out. The corn's moisture was borderline. A sample run to town was dispatched. All machinery was ordered to halt. The radio call back was: "Pull out. It's no good." While we waited for a re-test, we behaved like unruly schoolchildren. We threw corn cobs at each other in the field and had sword duels with cut and broken pieces of corn stalk. The second moisture report signalled our day's shutdown. Me, Tommy, John, and Jake made a run to Don's Food Center, a small supermarket in Onida.

I was still at war with Jake. We were engaged in a friendly, ongoing conflict of insults and verbal jabs in public. I do not remember the exact context, but there was another in-joke going around that spilled over into the open that day. As we strolled through the food store, an utterly classless response to one of his barbs flew into my head. I let Jake hear it, loudly, in earshot of several customers. Jake was taken aback before he laughed and proceeded to go at me again. When we stepped out the front door, we spotted a car over by the county courthouse across the street. It was occupied by a local personality who we'd had a run-in with during summer harvest. Our party of four went quiet for a moment.

"That is him?" one of the boys asked.

Another replied: "Yeah. That's him alright".

We smiled as we drove off. The individual across the street in the car did not.

The next morning's corn moisture kept the crop off-limits. With no harvesting that day, we switched back to trucking mode. Back at camp, I moved around one of the fuel-carrying tandem trucks to transfer some diesel over into another tank. That truck didn't have the easiest gearbox to operate. When I moved it, that time, it was a grind-free exercise. I felt a lot more at ease in that truck than I did the last time I shifted it. In the afternoon we got another trip to Pierre. The barber shop was closed. We were heartbroken; we wouldn't get to chat with the girl who worked there. In fact, we might not ever see her again. To ease our heartbreak, we went down to check out a nearby casino.

Some of us, who were of age, went in. Tommy almost cleared the place out with his luck on the 'chicken house' game, and my luck with the Asian-themed machine proved profitable. Several common forms of gambling are permitted in South Dakota. The state has a history intertwined with the practice of betting money for a thrill. That casino was more like a casual, low-key sports bar with poker and gaming machines, as opposed to a flash, glitzy type of establishment, like the kind you might find in somewhere like Las Vegas, Reno, or Atlantic City. It did, however, serve free coffee, pop, and pretzels—three of life's simple pleasures. Even better enjoyed when having a punt, which I like to do from time to time.

Supper that night was the Cattleman's once again. The place was crawling with locals that night. I think there was a memo for every other pretty girl in the state to convene at the restaurant that evening. We ate, drank, got our chat on wherever we could, and made a real night of it. Cattleman's really is hard to beat. A bonus that evening was we enjoyed pre-supper and nightcap drinks in the reclining chairs out the front, overlooking the water. It was perfect.

After a cruisy 0830 breakfast, we hit a test-cut and sample, which came back fine, and hooked right into it. I'd purchased Creed, AC/DC, and Red Hot Chili Peppers albums at Walmart the day before. They got a good workout in my tractor that day. As well as loading up on the coffee at breakfast, I deleted a cold can of Monster Energy Coffee I'd picked myself at Walmart. I was energized. I pulled up alongside a truck to unload. 'You Shook Me All Night Long' was playing in my cab. I was plodding away in my own little world, right before my peace and serenity were shattered in an instant. Jake sounded the truck horn and let it fly for about ten seconds straight. I jumped out of my skin. When I turned around I saw Jake and his infamous grin, laughing his butt off. I knew I'd miss Jake and his juvenile antics. We got on well from the word go, and he became a good buddy of mine. It was one of many occasions on which Tennessee Jake made Harvest 2016 that much more fun. You never knew just what that mad, southern country boy would come out with next!

That night marked one of the last episodes of Cory's video-recorded push-up sessions. Those sessions took place in a truck and machinery shed just behind the area where our trailers were parked. After a session was complete, we would typically wait around a few minutes to catch our breath and refresh ourselves with a pop or beer. The shed floor became a common area of sorts where we'd just sit around and shoot the breeze, play cards, and drink. I ventured out back towards the trailer to go and grab my phone and another beer. I walked around the other side of the shed to reach the trailer quicker. As I rounded the corner, I heard a sudden inhalation of breath and a clobbering sound. I whirled about, drew my knife, and stood on guard with my forearm high and a wider stance to defend myself. I'd run into a startled deer which ran off into the night. Oddly enough, it was only feet from where I'd seen the 'mountain lion' creature earlier on.

The next day was Sunday. South Dakota is a predominantly Christian state. In South Dakota, worship doesn't stop for harvest time; harvest stops for worship time! We had a sample to run in to the elevator, but the depot wasn't quite open yet. I was sat waiting with Cory and George. We discussed church, aspects of Christianity—the common faith of the three of us—and the passages that describe the finding of Jesus in the temple. We remarked on how the elders and teachers in the temple, as described in the Gospel of Luke, must have been captivated by and in awe of a boy, aged about twelve, who had them all listening with bated breath as his earthly parents searched all over for him.

It still wasn't quite opening time yet, so I suggested to Cory and George we steal a quick coffee run. They agreed. It was about a two-minute trip to the gas station at the corner of 185th Street and 304th Avenue. As George was filling his coffee flask I stood just near the front counter. The woman at the counter, who I didn't recall seeing before that morning, said to me: "Hey, do you wanna sweat?" She was easy on the eye and addressed me with a mischievous, almost sultry tone.

I replied, "Yeah, sure!"

She said: "Well you should get a cup of Highlander Grogg coffee, then. That *will* make you sweat!"

I nodded and agreed.

I've been drinking coffee on and off since I was about seven years old, so even at twenty-eight, my system was well-adjusted to the effects of coffee. I didn't get the hot sweat I was promised, but I had to say, that coffee did have some kick to it.

The cutting didn't happen that day so I went for a walk. It wasn't too cold, and I wanted to see what was happening with the John Deere fleet down the road and around the corner. Just like they did in Minnesota and Kansas, in South Dakota, people would stop and check on me when I was walking. I'd tell them "Yeah, just out for a stroll, all good, thanks!" and they'd happily go on with their travels. I put it down to two things. One: not many people go walkabout on the roads there. Two: South Dakotans are friendly people who will generally go out of their way to help you and ensure everything is ok. I'd just enjoyed a scrumptious Mexican supper, courtesy of Sue, and it was still light out. As I walked further from camp, I bumped into a gentleman who had been on the land there all his life. He and his family apparently owned much of the land nearby that the other family, who we were working for, didn't. He walked me through a concise but informative history of the farmland where we stood. In fact, we stood a few hundred feet from the house he was born in. I thanked the gentleman for his time and the chat, which I really enjoyed.

We fired up the machines and had a crack at the final corn section the next afternoon. Rob correctly predicted that, at first, we'd be ok, but as we ran into the slightly wetter stuff in the middle, that would be where things would end. We had to call it quits under an hour in. Back at camp, we discovered a load printout from the tractor's onboard computer had been left behind. I volunteered to shoot down the road to the field to grab it. 'Dirty Deeds Done Dirt Cheap' by AC/DC came on Capital City Rock just as I started the Dodge pickup's Cummins engine. I drove a hair slower so I could appreciate the Bon Scott classic front to back. Little did I know, I'd just driven to and from my machine, Tractor #1, for the very last time.

In vintage form, Jake managed to lighten up what would have otherwise been a chilled, uneventful afternoon at camp. A crew member received an unsavory text message from someone who he didn't expect would write such a thing. Unbeknownst to him, Jake had hijacked the other party's phone and sent the message. The crew member was bewildered. He looked around and responded in kind, via text with a two-word answer. The other crew member, equally stunned, messaged his counterpart back to quietly ask what on Earth was going on. In the supper line, when neither of the parties involved were around, Jake burst into laughter and revealed what he had done. The rest of us sniggered. Until now, I'm not sure if either of the texting messaging parties ever found out exactly what happened or who was behind the tawdry stunt.

Annandale, Minnesota

October 2016

A day or few earlier, Kelvin had been shipped off to Minnesota to work for another client of Rob's, not too far from the Holland Harvesting headquarters in Litchfield. The word that morning after breakfast was that I was soon to be deployed with Kelvin to help him knock the job over. Kelvin and the farmer had everything but a grain cart operator. Right on cue, Rob came in the trailer and told me to pack my gear and get ready to head back to Minnesota to fall in with Kelvin. Rob told me the farmer had 'lots of green tractors'. Rob knew I was a John Deere fanatic. I think the decision to send me to Minnesota worked well for him; he'd get to keep Tony, the faster and more skilled grain cart operator, and he'd have me working on machinery I was familiar with, alongside Kelvin, a crew member who was a good buddy of mine. I packed my gear and rolled out in the Lincoln.

The night before, I had received a strange, eerie message from Kelvin. Throughout the season we sent each other memes, comments, jokes probably best not aired on the two-way radio, news and gags from New Zealand and Australia, as well as all sorts of stupid and memorable communications. All Kelvin sent me that evening was a quote from Psalm 23, verse 4: "I walk through the valley of the shadow of death". He attached no image, context or explanation. I replied and messaged: *Are you ok, man?* I never got a reply. Later that evening, across the state line, I would discover why Kelvin sent that message.

Mentally, I never really said goodbye to South Dakota. I had to leave it in such a hurry about a week before I expected. I'd been in the state long enough to know our end of it well. In the United States, on that harvest, it was my home. If I'd had the time, I'd have gone for a lap around the nicer fields we cut, by the Fireside, and once again around and through the Onida township. But I had a destination to reach and a timeline to stick to. There just wasn't time. I felt a tinge of sadness as I drove west. Harvest wouldn't be the same again. The core group of 2016 was now fragmented. It would all change. I had Snapchat and messaging to stay in touch with the guys constantly, which I did, but I really missed being part of the group, even though I'd see them again in a week or two.

Back in Minnesota I linked up with Kelvin and headed out to join Tom, Rob's client. Tom had given me and Kelvin the bottom story of his home to share. After spending five-plus months in a trailer-confined bunk bed, having a whole room to myself was quite a novelty. As for the room, well, it kind of explained the Psalm-quoting message Kelvin had sent. He later said he'd forgotten to send the image with the text message!

I thought I was pretty obsessed with John Deere as a brand. I had nothing on this guy! Throughout Tom's house, he had John Deere pictures, key hangers, wallpaper, models, rugs, a pool table complete with matching John Deere billiard balls, and more. I was blown away.

There are John Deere outlets in existence with less merchandise on the floor than could be found in Tom's house. It was all probably a little bit much for Kelvin, the Case IH man. No wonder he'd broken out a bit of Psalms to call on for some strength! Despite the increasingly cold and miserable Minnesota weather that was setting in, I could see a good time coming around the corner.

I woke up early the next morning and met Tom. We discussed our mutual appreciation of Deere & Company. Tom showed me more of his numerous models, collectables, and pieces of memorabilia from the company. He'd owned, or still did own, almost all of the machines he had die-cast models of. I was in awe. He even let me hold one of the famous golden keys, given to purchasers of new tractors. He discussed the John Deere factory interior, manufacturing process, and the world-famous museum in Iowa, one state south. That was someplace I knew I'd end up at before too long.

The corn moisture level was about right, so it was time to head to the field and crack on into it. I was given a John Deere 8295R model to run the grain cart with. It was new, clean and, most importantly, had a good heater. Kelvin was on combine duty in the #2 machine he'd used all season. Except this time he'd had tracks fitted to withstand the boggy, moisture-ridden Minnesota terrain. Swapping to IVT—John Deere's transmission alternative to the Case IH-built CVT—took a bit of getting used to. Thanks to my time with Cervus Equipment Manawatu in New Zealand, where I'd had the chance to drive a range of different John Deere models, it all came flooding back. I had that green and yellow machine darting around the field after Kelvin without delay.

To date, I'd only seen Minnesota in spring. In that corner of the woods near Annandale, well into fall, it was a stark reminder of how different one state's geography is to another. The Minnesota corn fields weren't that big for starters, especially compared to the mega-sized wheat, corn, and soybean fields we'd harvested in South Dakota. There were trees everywhere. The fields had gentle slopes, corn planted around sharper bends, dips, rises, and it was like they were all within a stone's throw of a lake. Minnesota vehicle licence plates have text which reads: *10,000 Lakes*. On my first day back in Minnesota, I reckon I saw about twenty of them. In general, I preferred the dead-flat, sparse, wide-open plains of South Dakota to the rolling, tree and lake-filled land of Minnesota. But I had to say, Minnesota in the fall was a pretty good-looking sight. I could definitely see the appeal of the place. Except for the increasingly harsh cold.

John Deere builds tractors that take minimal effort to operate. To change your ground speed, air temperature, radio station, light and beacon settings, or pretty much anything, you only need to move your wrist an inch or two. It's not hard to operate models from different manufacturers, however, several of them require you to move and reach around the cab more than you have to in a John Deere. The drawback is, for the less familiar operator, the buttons can look a bit samey and there's a risk of hitting the wrong one if you rush it. But if you know your way around the controls, you can belt out maximum work with minimal movement. In that 8295R I cycled through the FM frequencies and found several rock and classics stations bound to keep me entertained. I'd later discover that, like me, Tom was a fan of AC/DC.

Right as we were set to kick off the next morning, Kelvin called me over and told me about 'the bridge of doom', which lay at the bottom of the hill in the field we were about to cut. He'd just taken a call from Rob, who'd given him the details of what lay ahead. Rob had an intricate memory of every field he'd ever harvested. At the beginning of the day, Rob would call in and provide details and/or a warning about a particular feature in a field that was worth looking out for. Rob wasn't wrong. The bridge that day had clearance of barely a foot on either side of the machine. You'd have to really get it wrong to creep off the edge. Still, it was one to take it slowly on. The bridge wasn't exactly in highway condition, either.

The field that day was a Minnesota stereotype. It was full of good corn. It was muddy. It had hills, bends, slopes, and a small river. It was right next to a nice country house, complete with an old-style barn and a concrete stave silo. Nearby there was a large river that flowed into a sizable lake. The truckers did an excellent job maneuvering out into the loading area. There was little breathing room, and a few feet wrong from the driver would have probably meant a bogged semi-truck. The field wasn't that far end to end, but the numerous hills and bends meant getting back to Kelvin so he could unload before having to stop was easier said than done.

By the time I'd collect, unload, and head back, Kelvin would've just started flashing his three-quarter-full beacons. It was just like the wheat field near Balcarres, Saskatchewan, in Canada. While the hills added welcome variety and a challenge, they also slowed me and Kelvin down a hair. A wrong move with a machine of the size we were running could result in an overturn, or at the very least, a costly and time-consuming stuff-up—not to mention the endless ridicule we'd get from the guys for being the one who tipped over a tractor or a combine. After a day that flew by we stopped on the way back at the local Dairy Queen, as was tradition in Minnesota.

On the way to the field the next morning I swung by the gas station for a coffee run. I probably hadn't touched a coffee in almost a week. That was a rarity for me on harvest. The coffee run confirmed the observation we'd made, as a crew, back in April and May: there were a lot of hot women in Minnesota. We'd competed for phone numbers on numerous occasions in South Dakota and North Dakota, where we'd made the same observation, but given Minnesota has about 5,500,000 residents, compared to 850,000 and 750,000 in South and North Dakota respectively, the chances of a bit of promising chat at the gas station in Minnesota were, statistically, a lot higher.

The harvesting that followed that day was quick, but a little more straightforward than the days passed. Every field, no matter where you were or what you were harvesting, had its own little features and traits that made it easier or more difficult to harvest. That particular field had a good, flat-top area for loading and minimal points that slowed me down. Kelvin was able to move a little faster and, thankfully, I could push my machine quicker to re-join him at shorter intervals to keep him rolling at speed. The comfort of the John Deere, the coffee, the superb selection of rock music, and the pleasant scenery made the day zip right by. Even though it was just a one combine, one cart operation, it was corn. Nothing went too slow. I thought I was going about the same speed as I did with Tony when we were racing around after Rob and Tommy back in South Dakota.

Quote of the day went to Tom. The situation came about because I nearly got his tractor stuck. The only entry and exit point at one end of the field meant I had to keep driving through a wet spot that was, unfortunately, the only place where Kelvin could turn with a couple of his runs. Two big bits of machinery pushing through the same spot over and over was asking for trouble. It was about one in the afternoon when we'd almost finished with that part of the field. On my second-to-last run through the trouble spot, I felt the rear sinking in and the drawbar of my cart pulling me to one side.

I pushed my revs to the limit and quickly moved the steering direction to the safe zone. I was spinning and turning away for a good few seconds. I threw about half the field's mud up in the process as I struggled to make it out. I did, luckily. Kelvin slowed down for a moment, probably to Snapchat the carnage, and almost certainly to laugh as well. Tom saw Kelvin's machine near mine and yelled, on the radio, "Get that red piece of **** away from my green tractor!" As he roared into the handset, we could just picture the smile on his face. I laughed out loud and I bet Kelvin did too.

The following day started with a bonus coffee during a run to town with Tom. He needed some food and supplies at the supermarket, and he let me persuade him to call into the gas station for a minute to caffeinate. We punched out the final ten acres of the 'Town Hall' field without incident and pushed down the road to the next field with ease. Kelvin's machine blew out a much-needed component on the header. That forced a trip up the road to Kimball to replace the offending part. As soon as we could bolt on the replacement and down tools, we were back to it again.

We flew around that field like a pair of children on a supermarket sugar high and turned several hours into what felt like a few minutes. It was smooth sailing until the heater function on my tractor spat the dummy. A quick idle down and engine re-start had the hot air flowing again immediately, much to my relief. We pulled up for a field-served stew that evening. It was hot and fresh, a welcome relief, but I ate it so quick I almost burned myself. The cold didn't appear to bother the Minnesota locals who were working the harvest with us. It nearly turned me into an ice sculpture.

Our next mission was a field right by a housing development and a small farm setup. It only had one route to and from the unload spot, but apart from that, it was ideal to cut. It was pretty flat, had no more than one or two obstacles, and I had a consistent, clear line of sight to where Kelvin was at all times. I could even see whether or not his beacons were on. The unload area was on gravel. This meant unloading and maneuvering was an easy, stress-free exercise.

I eagerly listened to the local rock station. Its DJ particularly liked to play 'In Your Eyes' by Peter Gabriel and 'Photograph' by Def Leppard. Earlier I'd mentioned to Kelvin, on the two-way, that 'Dirty Deeds Done Dirt Cheap' was about to commence on one of the rock stations. Kelvin—largely an electronic and popular music fan—was still an Australian, so he appreciated a bit of AC/DC when it was around. The mainly silent radio broke into voice when Tom keyed it and said, "Paul, you mentioned AC/DC on the two-way radio earlier."

Thinking I was about to be told to keep non-work chat off the airwaves, I responded, "Ah, yep, that was me."

Tom said: "I tuned in and listened to that song too. I like AC/DC. Let's get it back on when they play another AC/DC song." We did, later on. Of course, it was the Harvest 2016 classic, 'You Shook Me All Night Long'.

In the morning, Tom's place and our field were frosted over. That meant we'd need to hold fire for at least an hour before getting on with it. We refuelled, blew out filters, and did some running maintenance while the frost melted away. With my extra layers, the thick, Carhartt jacket and hauling the fuel hose around over the truck and on the machines I managed to keep myself warm enough. The new field, right across the road from the previous day's one, was about average in terms of obstacles and ease of work. It did force an unload to the trucks on the road, which was easy enough. You had to make the operation quick and get it right the first time, while constantly watching out for approaching vehicles. The plus side was the surface was hard gravel, so there was no chance of getting bogged. The Maple Lake locals, bar one or two impatient jackasses, gave me plenty of room when I was out unloading on their local thoroughfare road.

The field's headland stretched right around next to a public reserve and a small body of water that looked, from where I was sitting in the cab, sort of like a swamp you'd expect to see in one of the southern states. Tom climbed in with Kelvin to accompany him around the headland, and to cut an area open so I could actually turn around and get the machine back out again. Sadly, we heard later in the afternoon there was a vehicle accident at the T-junction on the road, only hours after we'd moved on from that unloading spot we used. It was my understanding, at the time, that no-one was killed or seriously hurt in the accident. I hope that remained the case.

After another roading move further into the countryside the following day, we settled into a field right near a main road. It was next to a large elevator and bin setup. I pointed out to Kelvin more than once that there were several big, late model John Deere tractors parked out front where everyone could see them, and that we'd get a good view of them as we harvested the field. Our attention was soon diverted to a slick, modified jet black Chevrolet Silverado pickup truck. It stopped in the field to observe us. We did see the Chevy turn up once or twice again, although we never found out who was driving or why they kept coming by.

The 'Chevy' field was square-shaped, obstacle free, and lasted about as long as a Blizzard dessert from Dairy Queen in the hands of a crew member. Over the road, at our next field, there was more interesting machinery to look at. The person who lived next to the field, we heard, had been in the machine storage and hire business for some time. Right outside the house, only about fifty feet from the field, sat a shiny, blue International LoneStar truck, a flagship model from that brand.

It was about three hours into the day when Kelvin's combine threw up error codes. A quick call to Case IH was made and a diesel mechanic was on the way. I had to unload, idle down and park up. Right nearby, Tom was discing the field in his 9470R, a big, eight-wheeled, articulated John Deere machine that could pull a house off its foundations. I dashed over and asked if I could hop in on the learner's seat. Tom asked, "Wanna drive?" It was about the quickest 'yes' I'd ever said in my life. In minutes I was discing away at the field so Tom could have a breather. After we'd finished I got a photo next to that tractor, smiling like a small child at Christmas time after receiving a much-wanted present. That would be my final act of Harvest 2016.

Des Moines, Iowa

October 2016

A day or two after the last field with Tom, I bid farewell to Kelvin and the remainder of the crew. They would make their exits from Minnesota in the days following mine. I headed south with Jake over the state line to Des Moines, IA. Being in the Hawkeye State again was a time warp, just like the night before when I'd slept in the same bunk in the back of the Holland's trailer I'd called home months beforehand. My time had come to a close. With commitments ahead back in the Southern Hemisphere, I had to make my way down state, drop Jake off in Tennessee, and board a flight back to the corner of the world I'd come from.

The trip south wasn't without a highlight. With Jake, I called into the John Deere factory at Waterloo, IA, about two hours from Des Moines. On my last morning at Annandale, Tom had gifted me some currency for use at the factory's gift shop, as well as a John Deere golden key. That key remains one of my most prized possessions. I had a great time with Jake at the factory and museum. Although we had a road to travel, we could've stayed at that place for days on end.

Just like my work began and ended in south-central Minnesota, my time in the Midwest began and ended in Des Moines. Cold weather was gripping the region more tightly by the day. Harvest was over and done with. The season had wrapped up. All my friends had begun to travel home. I wanted to stay in the U.S. but my visa arrangements and the Federal Government ruled otherwise. It was time to go. The summer and fall harvests might have only lasted six months, but the memories of them will last forever.

Epilogue

Harvest America 2016 was a tumultuous, eye-opening, and rewarding experience that I will never forget. I learned countless new skills. I met people I'll be friends with for life. I got to travel to places that many people, even many Americans, won't ever see in their lives. I went with an open mind and got so much more than I bargained for. I found it difficult at times. There were days when I didn't want to be there. The work got stressful, and, at times, my highly-strung temperament didn't make life any easier for my boss or my crew. There were moments when I got so frustrated I wanted to hit the side of my tractor tyre with a ¾ drive wrench, and other times, often minutes later, where I laughed so hard I'd nearly do a rib. There were lows and highs. For me, the many highs far outweighed the handful of lows. Whenever I hear 'Sinking Like a Sunset' by Tom Cochrane—perhaps my 'theme song' for Harvest 2016—the memories come flooding back every time. Completing Harvest 2016 enriched and bettered my life in so many ways.

There are incidents, situations, and actions that did not make this book. They will forever remain in the Midwest and in the crew's memories. There are staff at swimming pools, Dairy Queen outlets, gas stations, and coffee shops who will never forget us: the gang of

Americans and foreigners who rolled into town to harvest crops and raise a storm. There is even a pizza joint, in an undisclosed Midwest location, that will not allow our patronage ever again.

There will never be another harvest quite like Harvest America 2016. Even if some of the crew reunite one day and have another go, it will be different from how it was back then. When I look back at 2016, there are a lot of what-ifs. What if I'd stayed back at Parliament and gone up higher? What if I'd adapted better and approached the harvest season differently? What if I'd used a different bit of machinery somewhere else? There are endless what-ifs. What I know is that, now, if I could go back in time and change it, I wouldn't. Not a thing. Harvest America 2016 was epic, unforgettable, and one hundred percent worth it. Thank you, America, I'll be back again soon.

Thank You

Harvest 2016 wouldn't've been possible without the help of many. To God, thank you for blessing me with the opportunity that you did, and for keeping me safe. To Rob and Sue Holland, thank you for giving me a go and taking me on. To Mum and Dad, thanks for your love and unwavering support. To my sister, Jen, thank you for keeping me updated with all the messages from New Zealand. To all the crew, thank you for teaching me all that you did, and for your patience when it would often take me several times to get it right. That said, I'm pretty sure we all had fun doing it!

To my editors, thank you for your time and effort. To The Hyphenator, thank you, too. There's no one in the game quite like you. Class of 2009 forever!

To Cervus Equipment Manawatu in New Zealand: Dan, Craig, Will, Tom, Milly, Simon, Vince, and the team, thank you for having me on and giving me a shot in Palmerston North and Feilding. Without the work experience I gained, I might never have boarded that plane to the United States. To my extended family: Rob, Nicky, Peter, Heather, John, Joss, Wills (to name a few), thank you for teaching me what you did about farming in my younger years.

And, to my cousins, Phil and Tom, thank you for your support and encouragement, and for going out of your way during the Northland farm runs of the early and mid-2010s to get me more machinery hours and experience. It all added up and helped a lot. Cheers.

About The Book

At 27 years old, Paul David Savage left his career in public relations and communications behind. He boarded a one-way flight from New Zealand to the United States to join a custom harvesting crew in the Midwest. With under twenty machine hours on tractors in his life to date, he had no idea just what he was in for. Join Paul and the crew who took him in for an action-packed, agricultural adventure through two countries and several states in a journey that only a select few ever experience. There is no harvest quite like the Great North American Harvest.

To South Dakota and Back: The Story of the Great North American Harvest takes you behind the scenes of custom harvesting like no other book does. It is the definitive account of this world-famous agricultural rite of passage that you can't afford to miss.

About the Author

Paul David Savage is a speechwriter, author, and heavy diesel equipment operator from Whanganui, New Zealand. Paul worked as a public relations and communications professional in private sector and government roles in New Zealand before moving offshore to work in the farming and mining industries. His work has taken him to the American Midwest, the Canadian prairies, and the Western Australian wheatbelt and Goldfields regions. Paul currently resides in Western Australia.

In mid-2018, Paul released his first book, *The First XV: A Decade-and-a-Half of Fonterra Co-operative Group*. It was the first book to chronicle New Zealand dairy export giant Fonterra's first fifteen years in business.

Harvest Photo Album

1. *The long road:* On a country stroll, you never know who you might run into! Litchfield, Minnesota.

2. *Before the carnage:* Two combines ready to be loaded. Litchfield, Minnesota.

3. *Camp-out:* Our campsite. Iowa Park, Texas. Photo: Kelvin.

4. *Evening run:* Going at it in Burkburnett, Texas.

5. *Rural America:* A typical intersection by a canola field. Kingman, Kansas.

6. *Loading and roading:* Augering out some canola on the road. Kingman, Kansas. Photo: Kelvin.

7. *Cutting in:* Clint and Tommy harvesting wheat. Kingman, Kansas.

8. *Night train:* Loading up in Haswell, Colorado. Photo: Tennessee Jake.

9. *Big time:* The enormous wheat field. Gettysburg, South Dakota.

10. *Night and nine:* What 9 pm looks like on harvest—our grain carts parked up. Onida, South Dakota.

11. *Formation:* A full park-up. Regent, North Dakota. Photo: Kelvin.

12. *Nicely done:* A well-cut field, right next to one of ours. Regent, North Dakota.

13. *The main drag:* Bikes parked up! Sturgis, South Dakota.

14. *Up on that mountain:* (L–R) Me, Tennessee Jake, Kelvin, Cory, Tommy, Philipp. Mount Rushmore, South Dakota. Photo: Helmer.

15. *Shake on it?:* Helmer and Lucy coming to an agreement. Indian Head, Saskatchewan, Canada.

16. *Bean there:* Taking down soybeans. Gettysburg, South Dakota.

17. *Big time:* A local elevator. Onida, South Dakota.

18. *The long row*: Harvesting kernels. Onida, South Dakota.

19. *Wrong one!*: No, the other Gettysburg! Gettysburg, South Dakota.

20. *Almost there:* Corn, nearly ready to go. Gettysburg, South Dakota.

21. *Kelvin of the corn:* Kelvin going at it. Annandale, Minnesota.

22. *Big iron:* Tom's almighty John Deere. Annandale, Minnesota.

Final Word

This book is dedicated to the memories of Rob Holland and Marc Delage.

Rob and Marc lost their final, hard-fought battles with critical illness in July 2018 and January 2019 respectively. The world of large fields, hard-working crews, and big combine harvesters will never be the same without these two men, who dedicated their professional lives to harvesting and farming the land.

Both Rob and Marc had lasting impacts on my life, and no doubt the lives of many other young men and women in the world of agriculture. There is not, and there will never be, a day that goes by when I do not think of the adventures I had working under both men.

Rob and Marc, may your souls rest in peace. You shall never be forgotten.

Marc Joseph Delage (2/27/1983 – 1/18/2019)

Photo: Janel Delage.

Robert D. Holland (7/5/1950 – 7/17/2018)

Photo: Sue Holland.

Printed in France by Amazon
Brétigny-sur-Orge, FR

19931942R00107